THIS BOOK is ⎯⎯⎯⎯⎯⎯⎯⎯⎯⎯⎯⎯⎯⎯⎯⎯⎯⎯⎯⎯⎯ master from men endeavouring to live the spiritual life or life of love. It explores the various difficulties, both inner and outer, a man must face when he truly embarks on a path of self-denial to discover something more real within. Always revealing, Barry Long's answers are incisive, compassionate, practical, profound and sometimes provocative.

BARRY LONG was born in Australia in 1926 and is now recognised as one of the leading spiritual teachers in the West. His teaching is radical in its practical application of truth to daily life and his uncompromising stand on the divine significance of the love between man and woman. It is Barry Long's unique addressing of the man-woman relationship with all its beauty and difficulties that has attracted many to his teaching. The core of this book challenges man not to dismiss, but to re-examine in a spiritual context his fundamental need for the love of woman, and then shows how he can use this love to purify himself in his spiritual endeavour.

TO MAN
IN
TRUTH

Enlightening letters

Barry Long

BARRY LONG BOOKS

First published 1999

BARRY LONG BOOKS
BCM Box 876, London WC1N 3XX, England
Box 5277, Gold Coast MC, Qld 4217, Australia
6230 Wilshire Boulevard Suite 251, Los Angeles, CA 90048, USA

© Barry Long 1999

The right of Barry Long to be identified as the author of this work
has been asserted in accordance with sections 77 and 78
of the Copyright Designs and Patents Act 1988

All rights reserved. No part of this book may be reproduced,
stored in a retrieval system or transmitted in any form or by any
means without the prior permission of the publisher

The letters in this book have been minimally edited with the names
and places changed to protect the privacy of the contributors

Cataloguing in Publication Data:
A catalogue record for this book is available from The British Library.
Library of Congress Catalog Card Number: 98-92188

ISBN 1 899324 15 1

Cover Photo: International Photographic Library
Photo of Barry Long: Ambyr Johnston

Printed in Singapore on acid-free paper

CONTENTS

FOREWORD   vii

TO MAN IN TRUTH FROM BARRY LONG   1

THE PRACTICAL LIFE

ENLIGHTENMENT IS NOW   15

YOU MUST COPE WITH THE WORLD TO BE FREE OF IT   41

THE INDIVIDUAL MUST CHANGE WITHIN   61

TRUE LOVE IN THE FAMILY   67

LOVE

EVERY WOMAN IS LIKE YOU — WAITING FOR LOVE   89

DO YOU LOVE HER ENOUGH?   107

LOVE BETWEEN MAN AND WOMAN IS INVARIABLY SELFISH   135

SEX IS GOD BLIND IN EXISTENCE   145

MAKING LOVE WITH WOMAN IS A PRIVILEGE   161

FOR MAN THE LOVE OF WOMAN IS GOD IN EXISTENCE   187

TRUTH

THE TRUTH IS NOTHING   203

FREEDOM IS A DAWNING   213

BE THE KING, THE MASTER OF YOUR SELF   229

WORKS MENTIONED IN THE TEXT   241

SUBJECT GUIDE   245

FOREWORD

The letters in this book were written during the 1990's by men of all ages from around the world. Although some of the letters are declarations of spiritual realisations, most ask Barry Long for help and clarification as the writers endeavour to live more consciously. The men who wrote the letters were familiar with the principles of Barry Long's teaching through his meetings, books, tapes or videos and were trying to make the truth real in their daily lives. The letters reveal universal truths about the human condition and the way to be free of it. The truth in essence speaks for itself and in these pages there will be much of help to men who are spiritually motivated but have not come across Barry Long before. However Barry Long's message is radical and non-traditional and to give context there follows a brief outline of his teaching.

What is Barry Long's fundamental message to any man who would be free or who has a yearning to find God or truth within?

Firstly, Barry Long's teaching is a practical one. He does not tell you to go to the Himalayas or withdraw into an ashram or sangha. Rather, he teaches the individual that by mastering his outer circumstantial life, 'getting his life right' where he is, in the busy world of family, friends and work, he will start to generate the power of a more profound inner spiritual perception. 'Getting your life right' is to intelligently address the areas of your life which disturb you, often your relationships with others, and take practical steps to eradicate the disturbance. Barry Long also stresses that self-denial and the dissolution of negative emotions are essential to the cultivation of inner stillness, detachment and ultimately God realisation. Many of the letters in this book show how these principles are put into practice. But perhaps the most radical aspect of the teaching is that the core of 'getting your life right' for a man is contained in his relationship to, or love of, woman. Barry Long teaches that both man and woman can reach the inner state of love of God through the one practice of loving each other rightly. Right love between the two has the power to transform the life and consciousness.

What is right love? When Barry Long speaks of love between man and woman, he is not referring to the sentimental notion that passes for love in our society. He is speaking about love with intelligence, a love which puts honesty first. Honesty in love is for a man and a woman, in the first instance, to see that they are only together in a love partnership to enjoy being together. Any negative emotions in either of them will take them from the state of love. The task is for them to intelligently examine and dissolve any emotion that arises between them. The honest facing of the fact will in time help free both from their unhappiness and allow them to go deeper into love. This love will be more impersonal and divine than ordinary love because they have put truth, or honesty, or God before their personal positions or personal love of each other.

Barry Long stresses that the fundamental fact for a man to face is that what he loves most in existence is woman. How is this demonstrated? By the fact that man consistently thinks about woman and that in any spiritual practice he undertakes he will sooner or later come up against his thoughts and emotions about woman. Once a man can realise that he truly loves woman, then he can learn how to give up his selfishness for love of her and start to bring the principle of the selfless or 'noble' man into himself.

Man as he is today is distracted, distracted from God and his divine nature. He is distracted by his attachment to his drive into worldly activities and he is distracted by his sexuality. In other words he has left his love. On his way back to his love he must give up his errant sexuality: his excitement, his lusting, his sexual fantasising and his masturbation. This is all part of 'dying for love' which enables him to transform his unconscious sexual urge into love in the act of making love. The right love of a woman will help him do this.

Barry Long encourages man to love woman as one-pointedly as possible. He teaches man to 'take a woman on' which means to stay with the one woman and love the past hurts and pains out of her. For the other side of this equation is that woman in her essence is one hundred per cent love but she has been seduced from this knowledge by man's sexual corruption of her. By giving up his sexuality and putting his worldly activities in their proper place — after his woman, not before — a man will then have the power to love his woman through her emotions, so that she starts to realise the love which she intrinsically is. He will be purifying her and making her more beautiful, restoring her to her original nature. As all this can only be done by a man becoming more and more selfless, the result is that in freeing her he frees himself.

If a man can go deeply into love in this way, shedding all he thought he was or held dear, apart from love, it is possible that he can realise the principle of Woman, behind the form of the woman he is loving. This principle is love or the dynamic nothing which can also be called God or truth. And this is where Barry Long's teaching differs from any other. Most spiritual teachings are teaching man to realise God or truth within himself through meditation, celibacy or some other traditional spiritual practice. To Barry Long this is the realisation of God or truth out of existence and is only half the story. The missing half is the realisation of God or love in existence where it is most needed. By man one-pointedly loving woman, which requires giving up his negative emotions, he can simultaneously realise the divine principle in existence and the divine principle behind everything, out of existence.

As Barry Long introduces his teaching of love to people around the world, the women in the audience often immediately recognise the truth of his words. They have never heard a man speaking of the reality of love in such a way before. It is profoundly relieving and affirming. Initially for the men it can be threatening and challenging, for they are uncompromisingly confronted with all that they have been getting away with for millennia. As the men and women practise living the truth they've heard, more men begin to get the message and the idea of the 'noble man'. Today there are many men endeavouring to live this way, and as some of these letters testify, man has begun to realise a more profound love. This book is dedicated to that noble endeavour, with gratitude to the men who contributed their letters.

Jade Bell, Editor

To Man in Truth
from
Barry Long

The first thing an ordinary man has to do to help him realise his spiritual yearnings for God, truth or enlightenment, is to examine his everyday life. He has to see where he is wasting his energies on distractive activities, and start making changes.

Every man has inside his body sufficient energy to take him through to the realisation of truth or God — God realisation, as it's called. For God realisation is the original natural state of man. But over the thousands of years of increasing interest in the distractions of the mind and the world, man has in most cases lost the state and the keen spiritual perception that goes with it.

Within man's daily life there are various habits he has to identify. He has to really see for himself that each is a form of distraction. For instance, he may have made a habit of talking too much, or frequently phoning his friends to see how they're going. He does these things because he can't stand the silence that is natural in him and because he can't stand to be alone without a constant supply of information. The habitual reading of newspapers, the regular listening to the radio or excessive watching of TV, all fall into this category of wasting valuable energy.

There are also his emotional reactions which disturb him and others and destroy his spiritual energies. Anger is one of the most destructive. He has to gradually withdraw from this emotional habit. He does this by genuinely seeing that there is no excuse for anger: he is either trying to do the impossible and getting angry about it; blaming somebody for upsetting his life which means he is not responsible for his life; or he is stubbornly trying to get his own way when the situation doesn't allow it.

The man has to look very closely at his relationships. As a beginning, he has to ask himself, 'If anyone I love died or left me would I be in pain?' If the answer is 'yes' it means he has an emotional attachment to that person; for it is attachment that causes pain, not love. He is dependent on the person and therefore they have the power to hurt or manipulate him. Such attachments destroy the man's spiritual power; while they exist in him he can never really be free. So he has to start withdrawing his emotional dependence on people close to him. If it is his mother for instance, and he is terrified of her dying, he must stop phoning her every day or week when there is no need.

He must also examine his work and see whether he's a workaholic and what that is doing to his love-life. When he complains, 'I'm so busy', is he lying to himself because he's really enjoying the momentum and excitement — even the problems? Is he aware that he's on an endless continuity wave that closes him off from much of the rest of his life?

Work is one of man's main distractions. If he gets too immersed in it he won't really be able to be with his partner or children when he gets home. Half of him — his mind and emotions — will be on the momentum of work. His attachment will not allow him to leave it behind: for what you are attached to obviously follows you.

Also, after what he calls a hard day at the office he is likely to need a drink or a drug to slow him down and relax him. Really he should have already slowed himself down and been relaxed at work instead of getting emotionally identified with it.

As he gradually withdraws from these many distractions in his daily life, the man's self is going to play up. His and everybody's self consists of a block of resistance to any form of spiritual discipline or self denial. It is the opposite to the pure intelligence and goodness of the man. Faced with such intelligent action his self will feel restless and threatened. His self loves him to be distracted and doesn't want him to have the extra spiritual power that is available when he learns to contain the energies he's been wasting.

That power takes the form of a greater authority which the man realises is coming into him; a greater sense of being what he is. He will not give in to people's emotional demands as he used to, either in his love-life or in the family. He will get a right aloofness from it all. He won't be dragged into emotional situations because the people around him will know that's not his game any more. For instance, he won't argue with anyone. He'll say, 'I don't argue. I just look to see the fact for myself.' Eventually he will say, 'I don't discuss things. You can ask me a question and I will reply as best I can, but I'm not into discussions.' Discussions solve nothing in the spiritual life; what counts is action.

The man will continue to love the people close to him, not according to their expectations, but according to the truth in him. As he does that, his inner authority increases and he has a greater perception of freedom. Living this way he sees more clearly through the distractions of existence in which he's been burying himself, to something indescribable behind it all. He starts to have intimations of 'the one', the one unnameable Being behind everything. That's another name for what I call God, life, love or truth. He will then have quieter moments, stiller moments of communion with that in his own being.

What I have described is a process of containment to develop a spiritual consciousness. It is the troublesome and distracting self that has to be contained. The self is a hard lump of emotional cunning that has formed in the subconscious out of all the disappointments and hurts the person has experienced since birth, particularly those of a sexual nature. It is terrified of being seen for what it is and directs most people's decisions and reactions from the safety of the dark of their subconscious. Being an unhappy entity, its influence spoils good relationships and situations and inevitably makes choices that are soon regretted. Under the light of spiritual scrutiny the self squirms and does everything it can to deflect the attention.

In any situation of self-denial or withdrawal, the self will be felt as an uncomfortable disturbance or restlessness in the belly, as everybody has experienced. It will try to move the man's body when he is being still; make him go for a walk, read the paper or turn on the TV. It will pressure him to think about giving up the process, to feel that he is being hard done by or even misled. The man must not give in to this. He's just got to stay with the self and not try to get rid of it, knowing that by containing it he is gradually reducing it. The authority he has gained is the intelligence with which he surrounds his self. But it must be without thought. And any pain is simply his self dying. He must not look for overnight miracles. He must remember that he himself made this restless old unhappy self and it is only right that now he should take responsibility for dissolving it.

One of the most difficult things for man (and woman) to grasp is how to withdraw from attachment to the partner. For this he has to introduce truth into the relationship. Normally people fall in love, make love and that's pretty well the end of it — until the misunderstandings and arguments start. When there is truth in the relationship from the beginning, the chances of conflict are reduced enormously. It means putting honesty before the love of the man or woman. The man must see that if he takes his emotions and negative reactions into a relationship — as everybody does — the partnership is going to be problematical. To avoid that he has to be prepared, with his woman, to give up his emotions and find out what causes them, in him and in her.

That requires a pretty intelligent partner, so in this I'm not just talking to man. Woman has to be honest, too. If he finds that she's emotional, in order to introduce truth or God into the situation he has to be able to say, 'What are you emotional about?' And particularly to ask this very rare question, 'What am I doing to you, or not doing, to make you emotional? If I'm doing something then I want to change that. I love you, so I don't want to make you unhappy. We're together to enjoy being together and if there is anything I can remove in myself that has come between us I will endeavour to do it.' Of course the woman will say and do the same, if she's a real woman. And neither must react in the old defensive ways of the past. So the principle is: honesty before love.

Otherwise you will have a dishonest love no matter how hard you try.

Honesty in love is the process of detachment. It brings reality into the partnership, reducing selfish and irresponsible emotional expressions. Each one takes responsibility for their own emotions instead of trying to put their emotions on the other by accusing or blaming them and saying, 'You're making me emotional'. That's ridiculous. Only my self makes me emotional.

A man endeavouring to live the spiritual life has to practise loving woman. For the essence of woman is God or love in existence. Every man knows that woman is what he thinks about most throughout his life — from boyhood to the time of his death. He might say he doesn't want woman but he will still think about her. He will have thoughts about how he needs or wants to love her; or what he would like to do with her body — he's always thinking about that. This is true of all men. It indicates that the truth of love for man must be in woman. However, the one major obstacle to his loving her is his sexual lust for her. Now, how does he get rid of lust?

He gets rid of it by loving her physical body. I said loving her not sexing her. Love is utterly different from sex, although love is expressed through the sexual act. To love a woman is to enjoy her. And I don't mean just to enjoy her for five minutes in physical lovemaking. First man has to see he loves being in the presence of woman for the pure sensation of that enjoyment — holding her hand, walking with her — without any thought process. Any thought process about woman turns to sex. When the physical woman is in front of him, does he need to think about her? No, you only think about what's not immediately present. If he does think or fantasise about her while she's there, he is lusting, not loving. And if he thinks about sex with her when she's not present, he's still lusting.

The man has to be able to see the beauty of her. If there wasn't this recognition of her beauty somewhere inside him, why would he think about her all his life? He has to see her intrinsic beauty instead of his own habitual sexual wanting to possess her. He has to realise that he loves her because she has an indescribable essence that he, man, does not have. She is his missing love, the missing expression of God in his existence.

Man cannot love a woman truly — as woman needs to be loved — while his sexuality is rampant. That means while he excuses his sexuality; while he watches pornographic movies, reads pornographic magazines; while he excites himself with photographs of naked women or parts of her — and any of that sort of distraction instead of loving a real woman's body; and while he masturbates which means having sex with himself. Also, man cannot make love to a woman while he is fantasising about her or another woman because that's introducing a phantom woman into the relationship. Man often does this to keep his self excited but it means he's not really there, and he's not loving. He has to give it up.

Something man does habitually is to look at women in the street. In doing this he is subconsciously feeding his sexual self. His sexual self actually turns his head and looks out of his eyes at a woman, often before his attention has even noticed her. The sexual self is faster than the mind.

There are two ways of looking at a woman. One is to see her beauty. The other is through the sexual self which has a phantom affair with her in a glance. He's got to give up looking. He's got to go through a stage where he actually denies himself the right to look at women in the sense I'm talking about. It may be said that that's suppression. But it's not, because he knows what he's doing — he's practising containment. Suppression is when you feel as though you're doing something because somebody has made you do it.

Woman of course often dresses to attract man's attention because she has a sexual self too — due to our sexual society. Some women go to excess and exhibit their breasts more to make them more obvious to man. A man trying to give up his lust has to turn away and not dwell on such a woman as he would otherwise have done. If a naked woman walked down the street, all the men would be gaping for as long as they could see her. But the man practising love would say, 'I'm not going to do this habitual thing that most men do in their unconsciousness. I won't look any longer and indulge my sexual self.'

I teach that it is important for man, as soon as possible, to stay true to one woman and take her on. This helps to bring him to his senses and out of his imaginative sexual mind. The key is that he takes her on and together they practise honesty first in their relationship (as I have described) and discover how far they can go together into the mystery of love. If a man still wants other women, how can he take on one woman? He can't. He's not mature enough yet. Wanting other women, he will be restless and discontented; or he will dishonestly pretend that all is well and because it is not, emotional friction will arise between the couple — a common cause of disharmony in relationships.

It is imperative for a woman, once she is impersonally mature enough, to have her man's total focus. But he will not be able to give her this while she is still distracted by her emotions and the lure of the world of experience. Woman has been so disappointed, so wounded by man's itinerant and casual loving of her, that despite what man and woman think, she cannot yield her love — the essence of her body — to him completely until she knows that he truly loves her. When she realises that — it is a deep psychological subconscious place — she can give her extraordinary divine energies to him in their lovemaking. These rarely invoked energies are the God coming forward through the woman. But while he is half-hearted in his love he cannot bring her or himself to the consciousness of this God within her.

The purpose of physical love between man and woman (who are the dual embodiment of God in existence) is for her to give him what he can never have on his own — the glorious female essence that lures him all his life. This divine energy purifies him immensely of his restlessness and negativity, as it does her.

I have described man who truly loves his woman as a noble man. He is noble because he is willingly dying to his own notions of love and independence. He is in the process of realising the consciousness of God or truth in his woman and in the reality of his own love. A quality of love or truth shines through him. Whatever he is called upon to do, there will be nobility in his action. For instance a noble man can love his children rightly because he is not attached to them. He speaks to them from a place of divine or impersonal love beyond the fluctuations of clinging and selfish human love. A noble man is he who reveals the human spirit in love, in looking after the sick, in caring for the suffering, in sacrificing himself in wartime or simply not allowing his unhappy emotions to sully love. It's all a matter of love.

So, the key to man rising within to the wonderful heights which the spiritual life makes possible is to first identify the distractions in his daily activities that are consuming the precious energy he needs. If he is honest, these are always there to be seen immediately in front of him.

He must not look to absolutes, to God, to enlightenment as something to be achieved. If he does he will overlook the immediate distractions that are impeding him — and continue on a futile search.

When I was a young man I used to go fishing off the surf beach of an evening with my first father-in-law. He was catching all the fish, and good ones too. I said, 'What am I doing wrong?' He said, 'You're doing what most people do. You're throwing out too far. You're throwing over them. The fish are right in close at this time of day.'

THE
PRACTICAL
LIFE

Enlightenment is now.
Now never ends.

Dear Barry

A question arose in me regarding a statement you made at a recent meeting, 'there is no light in the universe but starlight'. Is there nothing else that comes from within us beyond the senses that appears like light? En-lightenment? This has sometimes been described as being like the light of a million suns.

Your statement that man is ninety per cent love and ten per cent something to do seems to me right on. Whenever I have the urge to dive deeper within, I can always feel that 'something to do' which takes me away from 'it'.

In my life I have never known or found what I am supposed to be doing here. My life was a nightmare of school and confusion until I first found love at fifteen, a love very real at that tender age. I recall looking at this girl and feeling a rush of bliss or love so strong that I almost collapsed in the street as we walked along.

When I found Krishnamurti at sixteen many things fell into place. I often felt a bliss descending on me. I later discovered Osho Rajneesh. He seemed to have 'it' to a greater degree than anyone else I had met. By being in his presence I was able to go deep without effort. But it did not stay: I always came back . . .

This may sound as though I was window shopping. But I was not — just searching for what every man, woman and child is looking for, whether in shop windows or in church.

Once when I looked at a photo of Da Free John the same feeling happened: a descending bliss fell out of nowhere.

This is the real stuff that makes my heart feel right. All the other stuff of life — the beastly office, the bullshit, the ruination of the beautiful earth by man and his world — can all go to hell! Pre-sence, prior to the senses? Being in the present, is it being in the Presence? — in the moment of creation all the 'no-time'? Is that a key to the real? Not a method to be used but a way to live?

I am left with the question of what I should do in this world.

Alexander

Alexander

Thank you for writing and recounting as you did — it will help you to get moving when the time comes.

There is no light in enlightenment. There is no metaphor for it, certainly not that mischievous eastern-tradition statement, 'like the light of a million suns'. Enlightenment is now, uninterrupted every moment wherever I am. And please don't put your 'I' on me. Only the unenlightened would attempt to describe enlightenment as light. Light is light. Water is not two parts hydrogen one part oxygen. Water is water.

What are you supposed to be doing here? You're supposed to be doing your life. Do you really think you can do anything you're not supposed to? You will keep doing, or living out your life until finally, probably in your more advanced years if it is to be, you will realise, 'I am here to enjoy my life'. Amazing, isn't it? While you've got the vitality, mobility and zest you can't enjoy your life for long — you live in spasms, like a sperm struggling in pain and joy to reach the womb. And what then? The tryer, the wanter, the searcher, the believer, the thinker, the monitor, the speculator disappears. He who thinks he would have enjoyed the end so much, never makes it to the end. There is only now — which is why enlightenment is now. Now never ends.

Be of good cheer. Do as you do. You are working out your purpose. Do not be surprised if sometimes you feel you are nothing; that's part of the disappearing act.

◆

Dear Barry

My life is getting better and better and I have nothing to complain about, but once in a while a question mark arises in my head. I wonder if you could help me get rid of it.

The question is about when to use effort and when not to use effort. In your second Journal you talked about the parrot which is always talking and talking. And there you wrote that you can use no effort to get rid of the parrot but sometimes you have to use effort. So what do you mean by having to use effort?

No effort I can understand and enjoy. You and many other masters talk about the witness as being the key to freedom and that certainly is no effort. I'm really peaceful when I give up trying. Trying is very trying, as you once said, and I couldn't agree more, so where does effort become necessary?

Sometimes the mind starts running like an idiot and at those times your words echo in my head and I ask myself, should I try to stop it? Which brings me to another question: If I see myself thinking, is that thinking? Clearly I'm not lost in thought and yet I'm thinking.

Dear master give me the key to heaven.

Terry

Terry

You have to use effort to be free of effort. It is an effort to try to stop thinking but when you no longer think aimlessly, there is no effort. It takes effort to not get angry when provoked but when anger is surmounted, there is no effort. It takes effort to learn to drive a car or an aeroplane but when accomplished, there is no effort. Effort is the way of things until we get through the effort of giving up all our negativity and questions. It is an effort not to ask questions but when there are no questions, there is no effort. I trust you understand in your own experience what I am saying.

The witness can be described as the key to freedom because the witness, like any good witness, is impartial. The witness is free of judgment and choice. Where I come from even the witness finally vanishes. But to get to the witness in the first instance, to get beyond judgments and choosing, is quite a spiritual state.

If you see your self* thinking, you are not thinking. It is your self thinking. And you are not your self.

As thinking arises from the emotional self, thought will always be there while the emotions are allowed to control the responses to living. For that reason I urge people to get their life right. While your life is not right in any area, you will be emotional in that area. And each time you are confronted with that part of your life your emotional self will be disturbed and you won't be able to stop thinking about the problem. So get your life right and gradually the incursive thinking habit will diminish and worry, being intense thinking, will trouble you far less.

---

* Self: all the past hurts, disappointments and sexual traumas since birth — the pain of the human condition.

Also, thinking is an entertaining habit. People get bored with the reality of now and start thinking aimlessly which is a pleasure to the emotional self. You must stop aimless thinking as soon as you perceive it. Then there is no thought. So why do you start thinking again?

The key to heaven? To love God or Life or It more than my self.

◆

Dear Barry

When I have a deep emotional disturbance within me, usually fear and anger, it becomes so rampant and active that it gives rise to bad headaches and pains. I have diffi-culty containing the pain. Sometimes it's so powerful that I think I'm going mad. Should I focus on the pain to dissolve it — or should I focus on the good beneath the pain?

Keith

A week later he wrote another letter.

Dear Barry

I wrote to you last week about whether to focus on the pain or the good inside. I have another question about sex.

When I came across your teaching a few years ago, I practised everything you taught and I've been to see you in public about three times. I've recently come back to your teaching after being away from it for about a year.

I am also involved in a gnostic movement, a kind of Christian sect with a gnostic master. This teaching advocates various forms of sexual magic and ceremonies and the practice of seminal retention, to divert the sexual energies up the spine to awaken the kundalini life force until it reaches the centre of the brain. They say no-one can be liberated without this alchemy.

It is considered a sexual fall for a man to ejaculate, attracting the dark forces of the 'Black Lodge' on the astral

plane and incurring penalties from the judges of karma.
These dark forces can actually be seen by those whose
latent psychic abilities have been awakened.

Although I feel the gnostic teaching to be largely true, I
am not convinced of the absolute rightness of seminal
retention. Does lovemaking, the way you teach, encourage
the dark forces?

Keith

Keith

Your so-called masters are masters of complication, not
masters of gnosis, love or truth. It is these sort of masters
that the complicated human mind loves to become
enmeshed with. It gives a sense of purpose when instead
it is purely another form of entertainment and the
endeavour to get something — to get and not to give.

The so-called White Lodge exists only because of the
so-called Black Lodge. The notion of good exists because
of the notion of bad. Men's silly complicated minds have
invented both and continuously complicate the simple
truth by posing opposites. If there is hot there has to be
cold. If there is love there has to be hate. But in the truth
there is no opposite to love, except in man's mind, as
there is no opposite to God, truth or gnosis. Gnosis
means knowledge of the whole and there is no ceremony,
teaching or technique that can bring this about, except
the simple surrender of everything I want to God or love
within me.

So you keep shopping around for new masters and then write to me, the master who gives you nothing, for something.

I have nothing to give you, Keith, except the truth, and the truth won't satisfy you because you are looking to get and not to give. Instead of all these sexual devices of retaining the semen or losing the semen, of black forces and the need of silly ceremonies and beliefs, why don't you and your masters simply learn to love woman? When you all learn to love woman — how to give and stop trying to get — all your questions will be answered, the lust in you will disappear and your selfish and complicated concern with the kundalini will also have no meaning. When the kundalini focus goes and along with it all the techniques you are practising — because you are practising love of woman — you will find that the truth behind the kundalini will have in fact entered your brain, and you will then be enlightened in a way that your present selfish seeking can never be and never realise.

You tell me, as though it were some achievement, that these dark forces, lost energies, can be seen by people who've awakened their psychic capabilities. (Are you trying to awaken your psychic abilities like this, trying to get something? I suspect so.) But let me tell you that these so-called psychic capabilities are a complication of the simple truth of real vision, in other words gnosis.

You say at times you have a deep emotional disturbance within you, usually fear and anger; it becomes so rampant and active that it gives rise to bad headaches, tension, aches and pains. Do you not see, you silly man, that these emotions in you are the dark forces, the negative emanations released from your lost energies in following your lustful desire for power through so-called spiritual practice? Do you need special psychic capability, man, to see that you are these dark forces in those moments, that you don't have to talk about the Black Lodge in the astral dimension as though it were something apart from you — but that you are actually a very paid up and practising member?

You separate your fearful and angry emotions that cause you headaches by mentioning them in one letter and then go on in a separate letter (to hide the connection) about your involvement with yet another silly sect practising sexual magic instead of love.

Do you see your subconscious deception?

The way to rid the entire world and psyche of the black forces is simply to get rid of them in your own psyche by taking responsibility for them. My many tapes and books, my continuous talks and meetings show you the way to do this. But the first rule is to stop trying to get and to start giving.

◆

Barry

Can you tell me if I am on the right track to God?

I am trying to eradicate anything unreal and dishonest from my communication with people. I usually look at people in the eyes and if they say 'hello', I don't say anything but continue looking at them. If someone wants to ask me something or talk to me, I stop and respond or say nothing depending on what's inside me. I don't say 'please', 'thank you', 'hello', 'good morning', 'goodbye', or anything that seems false to me.

Many people respond badly to my behaviour. I don't intend to upset them or dislike them, but find a silent exchange more beautiful and more honest. I don't avoid anything to my knowledge. When I'm walking down the street I always look directly into the eyes of the person coming from the opposite direction. On the rare occasion that somebody responds and holds my gaze, I find it a beautiful exchange of honesty.

Henry

Henry

I in that body am in a phase of self-realisation which, if you have my tape on self-realisation, you will hear takes from thirty to forty years — if you're lucky. I in this body suspect that you have created a structure of truth which now has to be dismantled. Your being true to the truth, as you have seen it all these years, has served you well but now it has become an inflexibility, due to the lack of sufficient love of woman. Truth without the ongoing balance of love is intolerable in this matter.

So I suggest you stop looking into people's eyes in the way you have described. You are actually putting something on them, projecting your self onto them with the conviction that this is the truth; and you look to get something back according to your notion of what the truth is. That was all once okay. It was actually to break some other opposite structure that you had adopted in your earlier years. I suggest you try being an ordinary man again, that you say 'thank you', 'hello', 'good morning', 'goodbye', whenever that is appropriate to being your sweet nature; to giving the openness that communicates a love, that obviously at this stage of your self-realisation passes your understanding.

I suspect you are afraid of people. Start giving for a change. What are you trying to prove by looking into the eyes of people coming in the opposite direction? Why aren't you looking at the sky, or the tree, or the little flower in the garden beside the footpath, or smiling at the sparrows chirping from the gutters?

Cut it out. Stop trying to be something and to get something. There is only one truth and that is living it as my own life of being free from unhappiness every moment through the art of loving and giving.

◆

Dear Barry

I am a sixteen year old school student. Nine months ago I picked up your book, 'Meditation A Foundation Course', and haven't looked back. Following the directions in the final chapter I bought the tape 'Start Meditating Now' and have recently finished my first reading of 'Stillness Is The Way'. I am amazed by how true and how applicable these teachings are to me and my life.

As far as I can see, I'm making progress and I'm understanding more and more the further I go on. As I continue to read, the question of my age arises. Can you see any significance in the fact that I am only sixteen? Some people around me feel that maybe I'm too young but I realise that they have no knowledge of the subject.

At present, I spend around fifty minutes each time I sit in meditation, usually twice a day. Is this an appropriate amount of time to spend? Am I progressing through your teachings too quickly? Could you please recommend the next tape or book which would be best for me?

Nathan

Nathan

Thank you for writing. I suggest the next book to obtain is 'Knowing Yourself'.

You are never too young to love truth or God. And you cannot love either too much. But you must understand and continuously see life as it is.

At sixteen years, you are closer to the womb, closer to the beginning, than your parents and the adults around you. They have the experience of more years and in most cases this experience becomes an unnecessary burden to them, due to their emotional attachment to what they have been and done, or what they think they have been and done. You have not been and done much, relative to the adults. So in one sense you are freer than they are, more open and willing to hear; and yet in another sense you are limited, as all young people are, by lack of experience of years. This is the dilemma of youth everywhere. They feel freer and newer and see the older generations as fixed and inflexible. But as the young drive confidently into experience, thinking they will handle it better, they too become attached to the burdensome emotions and eventually merely replace the older generation without really changing anything.

The only way life on earth can ever be changed for good is for the individual to change himself or herself within. The course of the living of years is inexorably fixed, as I have described above. Nothing will ever change out there; it will just seem to. You, at sixteen, have a subconscious appreciation that something must be done beyond the normal. And what you are doing by meditating and reading and listening to my work will help to keep you in touch with the innocence, the truth of youth, which youth must by the way of things flee from in its drive into the world.

Right meditation helps to quieten the excitement of this drive in the cells of the body. Youth is a tightly coiled spring. And the years are its uncoiling. When you have reached an advanced age you will have uncoiled most of what you had to do by living since you were born. By that age I trust you will have gathered your experience and, by living the truth as I teach it, have shed your emotional attachment to the past, which is the only reason that the adults around you have not regained the innocence of their lost youth. This is the most difficult thing in the world to do, but that's life, that's what life's about.

So keep up the good work. You have to do what you do. So do what you do. And write to me in five years if I'm still around.

A year later Nathan wrote again.

Barry Long

Since I began reading your books and listening to your tapes, the clarity that has been reflected has been amazing. Lately I have been feeling much more whole and, I'm experiencing less and less confusion (which seems to be the same thing). I've come to a point where I don't want to go and sit in meditation for a certain amount of time each day just because I 'should'. I see the stupidity of imposing the repetition of meditation in order to break free of repetition. But what am I left to do? Am I not to sit in meditation each day?

I'm now seventeen and am still at school. With so many people around me, especially at school, I see the destructive aspects of the world flying towards me from every angle. Most disturbing of all, I understand that the stone I don't see is the one which is going to hit me on the back of the head and leave me unconscious on the ground with everyone else. So of course, I must remain aware, conscious as possible.

I've been drinking with friends at weekends for quite a few years. I have observed an appetite inside that has driven me to do this. No matter how many bad experiences I seem to have, the hunger continues. There seems to be the same hunger for other emotional experiences like art and a painfully deep craving for woman, which is not just a sexual thing. I know that suppression is not the answer.

Can you uncover the structure of these problems?

Nathan

PS After listening to your tape on death, it seems so obvious to me that at the time my body dies, the life simply recedes as it does in meditation or in sleep. I can see that life, being life, doesn't die: it just recedes and emerges as forms of life. Is this what is called the realisation of immortality? I get the idea that true realisation would be a stronger experience than this, even though what I can see is very powerful in its simplicity.

A week later he wrote again.

Barry

After writing to you last week about the continual craving to experience something new, I realised that I was dodging the central issue. Now I'm beginning to understand that this craving is not fundamentally a desire for drugs, alcohol or even music, although it has been translated into these forms. I think the factor which drives all of these is the longing for love, especially the love of woman.

Listening to your tapes and reading your books have helped me to be aware of my sexually aggressive actions. I still observe the evil inside of me every now and then but the imagery which used to present itself so frequently a few years ago is no longer welcomed. I am feeling more peace and stillness and an amazingly vital love of nature (which is probably a result of the imagery departing).

At seventeen, I haven't been in a sexual relationship yet but can understand what you mean when you describe woman's true self. I see her so often, in the different friends and people I know, including my mother.

This morning I was reading your book, 'To Woman In Love', in a bookshop. Although it may be directed more towards women, some of it affected me so strongly that I began to cry.

My longing is very deep. I now know the utter desolation which you have described. Sometimes in my patient moments the emptiness is gone and I feel content and good without any external cause. But always the emptiness returns. Do you have any words for a boy in this situation?

Nathan

Nathan

I have received your two letters and I'll make a couple of comments as you requested.

First meditation. You have attended one of my seminars, part of 'The Course in Being', and I remind you of what that teaching is. Although sitting meditation is okay if you need to do it, it is far more potent to practise being — being now. Being, you will recall, is a state of inner reflection on nothing. It is and can be practised with the eyes open walking around, pausing while watching TV, or pausing in any other physical activity. No time has to be fixed for it, you don't have to 'sit'. You be now.

You are a seventeen year old boy, but also a wonderfully perceptive young man. I suggest that you continue observing life as you have been doing. The fact of being seventeen or a youth like your friends, is that you have to gain experience. You have to drive into the world. Although you have a profound sense of reality within and the pause in the mind's activity that goes with that, you still are forced by the way of things to gain experience.

The fact that you were moved to tears by reading, 'To Woman In Love' reveals your deep sensitivity to woman's plight. Your longing for her will be answered in time, for loving her is an essential part of experience. Do it as well as you possibly can. Your letters show me that you have more love in your body than your mind can comprehend.

◆

Dear Barry

I would like to ask you about meditation. I've heard you say that not all meditation is right.

Before I came across your teachings, I practised Transcendental Meditation. I gave it up and practised your meditation for a year. Then I tried Raja Yoga. In this method you see yourself as a point of light between the eyebrows and focus on that. I found it quite good but noticed that it draws my attention into my head instead of my body.

The practice of celibacy in Raja Yoga disturbs me. I see the value of celibacy in gaining power over our emotional states but I believe that nature is the guide to spiritual equilibrium — through health by eating natural foods and through making love without sexual excitement.

The real reason for me taking up Raja Yoga meditation was that the eyes are kept open while meditating so that you can see others as this point of light. This kept me awake. While I was practising your meditation, I tended to fall asleep. Can you give me some guidance about Raja Yoga?

George

George

If any other meditations were more right than my own, I would not have given mine to the people. Raja Yoga rightly interpreted, is union with God through insatiable, one pointed desire — an all-consuming meditation or consummation hardly associated with points of light outside yourself or any other practice or effort. Transcendental Meditation must mean the transcendence of something — what? What is the only thing that can be transcended? Meditate on that day and night until you are the answer and you will be the one person who has truly succeeded in Transcendental Meditation.

You take up Raja Yoga, so you say, and then choose to ignore its precept of celibacy. How can you be so self-deluding? Can you eat half a tart without eating the tart?

If you knew instead of believing what the guide to spiritual equilibrium was, you would not be writing such a letter to me. You are looking to gain something for your self to add to your self — instead of practising meditation to shed your self, a courageous and very rare preoccupation. That is right meditation.

PS You fall asleep in meditation because you lose contact with the inner sensation in your stomach/solar plexus area. It is as though you started off looking at an object like a flower and then allowed your mind to unalign itself with what you were seeing so that it dreamed off into a subtle subconscious sleep. You must be more attentive to what you are doing. The mind will always choose to dream off or go to sleep until it is mastered. You can keep your eyes open while addressing the inner stomach sensation. The closing of the eyes is only necessary until there is sufficient attentive power to not lose touch with the sensation while the eyes are open.

◆

Barry

I have heard you to the depths of my being* and for this I am eternally grateful.

I have been endeavouring to live the divine life for several years. My question is: how do I make a shift in consciousness from the position my self takes to the place of my being? More specifically, how do I maintain this shift? How can I reduce my self enough to stay being?

I have been a cigarette smoker and have masturbated for many years. Last year I endeavoured to stop both. But, not working or having a partner at the present time, I find that I drift back into these habits. When I don't do either, I find that I have more energy and a greater clarity in me. I know that it is my self that motivates these habits and I find that I am not one-pointed enough to maintain my place of being. This also applies to self-judgment and the sticky, slow unconsciousness in me.

Am I right in saying that the more I go into Me**, even if it is through meditation, I will reduce my self and my authority will get stronger?

Words seem to be a very limited way of communicating. It has been a privilege to be in the presence of truth and love. I know that when you, the body that is Barry Long,

* My being: the fundamental state behind the senses and the body but because it's not sensory it can never be known with the mind.

** Me: the place inside every body where there is no negativity and where at any time we may register love, tenderness, joy and beauty. No negativity is ever registered in Me, only the good and the right.

Barry Long takes the people into being and Me at his seminars and public meetings.

has perished, the love and truth that I am will always be.
You have shown me so much more than I could ever have
found on my own in such a short space of time. In that
knowledge I will endeavour to live the spiritual life until
the day I die.

Greg

Greg

You have answered all your questions with the one
saying, 'Am I right in saying that the more I go into Me,
even if it is through meditation, I will reduce my self and
my authority will get stronger?'. The answer is yes. But
there is more to do and that is to be rid of the cigarettes
and masturbation for good as soon as you can. These, as
you know, disturb the body and the mind and make you
have to meditate instead of just simply being.

Your letter shows that you are willing and grateful to
God for what you have received. Such gratitude, frequently
offered, is greater than anything else you can do. Keep up
the good work.

◆

Dear Barry

I have listened to many of your tapes and would like to know what your thoughts are about Primal Therapy. Can it help you get into the unconscious?

Matthew

Matthew

A therapy cannot access the unconscious to the depth of uninterrupted God realisation. A therapy entails doing; and doing, in an effort to find the truth, will leave you still in the realm of the ignorance of the human condition. This despite the fact that you may dissolve some of your ignorance — but never all, as in God realisation. That perfectly natural but very rare state of consciousness is realised only by dissolving all of your self. And that is done by not doing.

Your self consists of all your negative emotions such as anger, resentment, moodiness, misery, self-doubt, self-pity, sexual fantasising, aimless thinking, trying, wanting and so on. Take anger. Anger, and any of the other emotions, are the doers. They move you by having you join them. The thing is not to allow them to move you by starting not to move with them, not attaching to them. They move (if they are able), you don't. By not joining in their doing, by doing nothing but being consciously present, you gradually separate from your self or selfishness and discover the reality that never moves. Once you are the immovable one, who uses no effort, the emotions — the self — gives up and you enter the perfectly natural state referred to at the beginning of this note.

The spiritual life is not a matter of doing, but of undoing — not giving in to the human ignorance that moves everyone and spoils their lives. The will to continually dissolve one's self — by not attaching to the movement of the emotions while being consciously present — eventually leads to the divine state of consciousness.

Until your letter I'd never heard of Primal Therapy. Any imagined similarity between what I have said and Primal Therapy is partial. As I say, Life or God realisation is a total transcendent and uninterrupted state. The price is complete dissolution of your unhappy, discontented, striving, seeking self.

◆

You must cope with the world
to be free of it.

Dear Barry

*I can't continue in my job because I don't enjoy what I do.
I'm frequently confronted by my dishonesty such as
taking off early from work or not working as efficiently as
I have in the past. It's a well-paid job which has provided
me with a comfortable existence and I've come back to it,
after leaving it once, in the hope that I could find more
fulfilment in it. But the situation hasn't changed and I've
spoken to my boss about leaving later this summer.*

*I don't have training or skills in any other area and don't
know what direction to take. There is no fear and no doubt,
though I realise that situations may be harder in what lies
ahead. I'm trying to live the truth as best I can. Please let me
know if I am being true to the situation or if some aspect of
what I need to deal with remains unconfronted.*

*There is this feeling of a 'greater destiny' that has been
an undercurrent of the past four to five years. This is
almost like a negative motivation as regards work in
general. What is action? What is inaction?*

Paul

Paul

You have not left yet. You talk of speaking to your boss
about leaving 'later this summer'. There is still a lack of

resolution. You have not yet reached the point of knowing that precedes decisive action. Do not be discouraged by this. Everything happens in its time. But I cannot tell you what to do.

The point is you say you cannot continue in the work (while you are continuing). Sooner or later it will reach a point where you *act*. Until then, nothing more can be said. When the discomfort is great enough you will quit.

So, you are being true to the situation as much as you can. You feel the need to enjoy your work, and this is not happening and it is increasingly intolerable for you to continue — but not enough yet.

When and if you do leave (and that is not to doubt that you will), whatever you do and whatever happens will indeed be another step, and steps, towards 'a greater destiny'.

◆

Dear Barry

I am a young man currently at university. I do not feel that my academic studies are altogether important. I spend more time trying to understand what you speak of, attempting to see the truth in my life — I long for this. In fact I do not feel good about my academic studies. If I could see a practical way, I would end all of them tomorrow.

I see many of the things which you speak of as the truth but I seem to lack the capacity to live them. Over the last few years I have been fervently attempting to absorb what you teach, to see the whole picture. It seems I have done well — I've given up many concepts, beliefs, ideas and notions that used to entertain me. But more disturbingly I barely have any idea of who I am or what is what and have withdrawn from the world, keeping only the most sparse contact. As I see it, my withdrawal has been from a growing fear rather than from awareness. I fear other people and what they think about me. This is what I've withdrawn from.

I realise that I must perform and live in the world but I do not know how to. I clearly want to 'get on' and live, facing each day and all that comes my way as I endeavour to throw away the old, welcoming the new. Yet every endeavour seems to be harder and the courage required greater than before.

I am struggling terribly right now and would really appreciate some input.

Jeremy

Jeremy

Why don't you start where you start your letter? Why don't you address your university studies and give them all that they demand? You have to do something in this world. If you changed it would not be long before you were discontented again. Your studies are important because they give you a chance to do something without giving in to your fluctuating personal likes and dislikes. If you focus on your studies and do the best you can you will find you will not have to spend so much time trying to understand what I speak of. The truth in life that you have been presented with is your university course. Now get on with it.

◆

Hello Barry

This is not an easy teaching. The longer I am with you, the more difficult it appears to become. Still, I recognise the truth of it.

I am deeply tired. The force has been taken out of me and it seems there is nothing else there. Force is a necessary element in my life in the world, my working life and, to some extent, my recreational life. The projection I need to control a classroom, debate issues in committee meetings, suggest ideas to colleagues and so on is not there at the moment. An effort of will can retrieve a part of it, but it hardly seems worth the effort.

It leaves the self floundering, as all I seem to be is nothing. This is not very reassuring for the rational mind and it makes day to day life at work quite difficult.

I would like to relinquish all effort. But this is a frightening prospect for what I am is a product of my efforts up until now. What remains when the effort is taken away?

Rick

Rick

Stick with it. It will change. But your resolve, your will to be nothing, will not.

It is the emotional body, the self you have acquired since being born, that is wearied and tired. It will struggle and play up until the end — but increasingly you will know implicitly the greater peace and stillness behind the struggle and effort. The effort is from the self trying to escape the nothing of your relentless focus on it, not your work and associated activities. You may not know this but it's the truth. You trying to escape is the self trying to escape — simply a case of mistaken identity. You being nothing, the mind by habit is still identifying with the something, the only thing inside you, the self.

Your whole spiritual life — living the truth which you say is so hard yet you cannot desist from — is the process of detaching your mind from its mis-identification; re-programming it in other words.

'All I seem to be is nothing,' you lament.

Well done. Stick to it.

PS Someone living the truth has to be with the school children — and you're he!

◆

Dear Barry

*This year has been a 'going through it' year. I lost my job
and with it the longstanding friendship of two men. At the
same time my partner left me and will soon be having an
abortion of what would have been our child. I will support
her until the situation is over. She doesn't want what I
want and I have accepted her decision regarding the
abortion and her declaration that she no longer loves me.
All these things I can deal with.*

*I have a problem with work and earning money. I am
forty-two years old and have never known or felt any
ambition in me to go and strive forth into the world to make
my mark on it. I have an apartment and the necessary
material things I need to live at this time of my life. However
since I lost my job I have struggled to find work and have
done depressing factory work.*

*Your teaching says, 'Surrender to life and life will
present opportunities and will take care of you'. But it isn't
enough. I know from experience that letting go to life and
not thinking about things does work: good or bad circumstances come along to teach me a lot. But, in the world,
circumstances don't provide food or money or a better
place to live and the opportunity for family life.*

*I can't accept my life at the moment. I am a creative
person and feel frustrated because I don't have an income
to be able to expand into a field where that creativity can
be expressed. I'm finished with wanting and trying but this
pressure of the world gets to me. I enjoy life but I have to live.*

Simon

Simon

So in the experiental life, the outer life, you have been 'going through it' this year. You have lost a great deal and have had to cope with those feelings — the loss of your job, two friends, your partner, her declared love and the unborn child. It is good that you will support her until the situation of the abortion is over. And I receive that you can deal with all that in yourself.

The current problems you are left with, you say, are work and earning money. At forty-two, it seems to me, you have entered or are into that stage of a man's life where what he has acquired, even his concepts and notions of life, are taken from him; or a complete psychological reorganisation is demanded. It's not difficult to see the reason for this seemingly disruptive process, sometimes called the male menopause. It happens because when a man reaches middle life he subconsciously perceives that much of what he has done and believed in was driven by the inexperience and immaturity of the young man in his late teens or early twenties, which now he is not. He is bound by past decisions and their consequences and in his maturing rebels against that bondage. He is not now the young man he was, and yet that young man set in motion most of the situations that he finds himself in today.

This transforming climacteric does not happen to all men, for some are so attached to the momentum of the past repeating itself as a consequential drive, that that is sufficient for them. They drive into life and out the other end without the pause that is necessary for a vital re-orientation.

It seems to me that you have sufficient money or resources to maintain things as they are. You mentioned creativity as well as money. The question I have to ask is, what do you want to do? What are you attracted to do that is creative? Don't look for the money; go for the creative activity. I say it is the lack of creative opportunity that is making you frustrated and not so much the money side. You are getting by financially so go and express your creativity without tying it to money. That expression will lead to fulfilment and possibly to some money as a consequence.

But I do notice that you refer to the 'opportunity for family life'. This seems a reactive statement following the break-up of your partnership and the loss of the unborn child. You have to leave that where it is. You have to do first thing first, and the first thing, as I say, is to express your creativity in no matter how small a way to begin with.

There is a niche for you, even without qualifications, if you will only follow your creative inclinations without other considerations. It may not happen easily, for you will still want answers to all the other questions in your letter which are really secondary. And that conflict will pull at you and try to distract your energies.

◆

Dear Barry

My particular problem is in controlling money and finances. This has caused many upsets, arguments and near break-ups with my wife.

I have been irresponsible and dishonest with money throughout my life. Although Julia and I felt the 'rock' of our love for each other, the emotions of my past kept me from being honest with her and myself. However, with her loving support, I managed to gain some control of my life, nearly pay off my debts and enjoy my family and home.

A few months later I acknowledged my dishonesty to you at a meeting in Colorado. After that everything fell apart: Julia and I had a massive argument about all my lies in the past, I lost my well paid job and a promised redundancy payment fell through. After being a well paid executive I had to face the prospect of living on welfare.

This was such a shock to me that I reverted to my old dishonest ways. It is only now that I am 'facing up' again but I feel despondent, directionless, unable to concentrate. How can I get control back? How can I be single-pointed when I don't know what to be single-pointed about?

Brian

Brian

First thing first. You must get out all your financial papers, savings books, accounts and sit down with your wife Julia and inform her honestly and completely where all the money is, what you have, what debts still exist and what accounts have to be paid and when. She is to do the same with any finances she has or is responsible for. You, Brian, must now be in partnership with Julia.

You have made a mess of your control of money. You have shown that you are not capable of handling the financial affairs efficiently to the benefit of all in the family. This is because you have the controlling or secretive instinct in you due to the past emotional hurts and pains associated with your parents and other earlier influences.

The most important thing in your life is to keep your family together rightly. While you and Julia are true partners you will get through together. Even if you 'go down' financially, you will fall together and in doing so you will have no problem, and nor will your children, in making any necessary shifts or economies.

You feel isolated, confused and splayed because you and the woman you have made your life with are not truly together. The currency of heaven on earth is love and the currency of the world on earth is money. It is all very well to say you love her but love has to be in the demonstration and to fail to share with her completely the financial management of the family is an act of non-love. You must look together at all aspects of the management of the family. You must agree together what is the best move, bearing in mind that you both have the good of the family, of the children and yourselves as a whole as the first consideration and *not* your own personal likes and dislikes or selfish wants.

Everything must be out in the open, laid on the table. In every case both of you together must ask this question:

what is the situation we are addressing? What is best for the situation? If you will both only address the situation you are facing, no matter how minor it is compared with the overall concern, you will find you agree on what is the best thing to do as the first move. Personal considerations vanish when only the common aim and the facts are considered together.

You are blocked in yourself by your own need to control. And it has led you to where you are today. Now give it up and be a partnership in all matters. And you will find that the train of events that began with your honesty at the seminar in Colorado, including the loss of your job, and the shattering of your financial severance expectations, were simply a just and right shaking out of your life for you to get it right for a new beginning.

You must be a living, working partnership in that house. It's up to you, Brian. You've got to do it.

But please bear in mind that I'm not telling you what to do. All I have said is purely guidance, which in writing to me you asked for.

◆

Dear Barry

I'm finding it very hard to dissolve the feelings of bitterness in me. I have been betrayed, taken advantage of and ripped off financially. This situation has occurred not once but twice in my life. I understand that I am responsible for my life and feel I could resolve my feelings better if you could explain why we create similar painful situations again and again. Why does it hurt just as much the second time?

Rod

Rod

'We' don't create anything. I, myself, create all my problems. Your trouble is you trusted someone. You cannot trust anything in existence except that the whole is trustworthy but not anything that you take out of context and attach yourself to. If you hold on to feelings of betrayal and resentment towards people and events, those feelings are likely to bring about a repeat of the same conditions. When you let go of such negativity there is nothing to repeat itself because living consists of having to face again what you haven't let go of in the past. *Life* is the peace and harmony of no longer having any need of past negativity.

Now wake up to yourself, wake up to the dream and start being true to life, the whole, not the particular.

◆

Barry Long

I am writing to ask you if there is any other way my partner Karen and I can pay for the Sydney weekend meeting, other than by paying $180 each. We are unemployed, by choice admittedly, but the available jobs lack fulfilment. As we already have debts we are reluctant to borrow money. Can we do any sort of work exchange?

I am confused and need some help. When I met Karen two years ago, her love for me awakened a great happiness in me. Spirituality, truth and love all came together. Now I'm confused and panicky. We've been caught in cycles of pain and struggle for months. I question my love for Karen. Sometimes I find her unattractive; other times I adore her beauty. I recoil from her anger and judgment of people and want her to be soft and compassionate.

I have sexual imagery in my head. When Karen fits with this, I feel satisfied; when she doesn't I question our relationship. I want clarity. I don't want to deceive myself or her. Is it just a matter of me being clear that I want to love her? I'm willing to face pain if that's necessary but I don't want to miss the love that I truly long for.

Alan

Alan

The problem in the first instance is not in your love for Karen, it is in your self. And because you are not right in your self that is going to make her angry, judgmental, frustrated. You have found the love for now but it is not working harmoniously and that's because you haven't got your life right, out there. If you had your life right out there, your love, the love between you, would be getting better, not deteriorating as you describe.

So yes, you are deceiving yourself. You don't want to work like the ordinary man and woman have to. You ask for a concession when all the ordinary men and women who have to work hard for the money don't ask. Who is more worthy, you who ask or they who don't? Should I make you special when I don't make them special?

Do you want to be with me now because your love-life is in trouble? If not why did you not put a little away or do some work to get some extra money in the time you've had before my coming to Sydney again?

You say you are ready to face the pain. Which pain is that? Will you face the pain of getting your life right and therefore your self right, as I am suggesting? Or is that too painful for you to face?

Woman must respect you, man. If she doesn't, she will give you a hard time to endeavour to make you wake up to your self or to what your self is doing to you.

I understand your position, I appreciate your honesty about not working because the jobs lack fulfilment (does not working give you fulfilment?) and that you offer some sort of work exchange. But I cannot offer you a concession. You must address your life as a whole; there are no partial solutions.

◆

Hi Barry

I have been seriously practising your teaching for a few years now. I'm making progress and doing well. I've been able to diffuse some difficult situations by following what you've said in your books and tapes. For that I'm really grateful.

I live the teaching every day and now I've reached a stage in my spiritual life where I feel I would like to be around other people who are living in the same way with the same interest in God, love and truth. I need that nourishment. I can't find that in the world and have never been able to finish a college course. I certainly can't find it in the workplace so right now I don't have a job. I would love to serve something real though. Can I come and work for you, Barry?

Jim

Jim

You can't be free of the world until you learn to cope with it. I suggest that as a spiritual exercise you get a job as soon as you can and work like ordinary people have to.

In working for others and with others you have to overcome the negative feelings and thoughts that are likely to rise from time to time. The best way to do this is to do whatever you have to do for a power greater than your self, that which could be called God. You are then not working for your self — remembering that your self is a troublemaker who will always resent any disciplined activity and seek an easy way out.

I am pleased you sense that you have made considerable progress in living the divine life and now it seems the time for the injection of a new energy of surrender into your affairs.

◆

Dear Barry

I often hear you define man as ninety per cent love and ten per cent something to do. I feel that you are somewhat denigrating about man's 'something to do'. Surely that's how God made it, so how can it be wrong?

Kevin

Kevin

It's what he does or builds with the ten per cent — a world like this or a world of love and justice. Which are you working at?

◆

*The only way life on earth can
be changed for good is for the
individual to change within.*

Dear Barry

I am writing to tell you how well I am doing. My life is good. I have no problem in my life. If something arises in me I look and see if there is any practical action I can take and if not I let it go (as much as I can in the moment).

I live an ordinary life and am currently in a loving and honest partnership and have a small child. Being self-employed I work long hours but my family can be with me as I work, so that is good.

In my life at any moment I am aware of a depth, or vastness in me. It is profound but not necessarily extraordinary. Often I could say that I am more that than this. Words fail me at this point. I know I am connected with being in this way and my life is moving me further into being. I often sense I am being guided by something wholly beyond my comprehension. I can do nothing of my self. More and more I am trusting that this is okay. That which is given to me is good and that which is taken from me is necessary and also good.

Dennis

Dennis

I am very pleased to receive your letter of good news. Not long ago I asked people, as much as possible, to give me the news about how good their life is and not to emphasise the problems. I did get a number of such letters but gradually the contagion of problems seems to have taken over the good in people's lives and I receive many letters expressing troubles.

Your letter is good from several points of view. First, you acknowledge the goodness of your life, which of course, is true in everybody's life once they have the profundity to see the good. Then you speak clearly of the truth of life you have discovered, that you have seen a vastness that is in the depths of you and although it is profound, it is not necessarily extraordinary. That is a wonderful truth. The hardest thing for people living the spiritual life to grasp is that enlightenment or freedom is now: that it is so ordinary as to be extraordinary to the normal thinking and speculating mind. All your profound insights are due, as you say, to your moving deeper into the stillness and consciousness of Being — the one Being that is behind every one of us and all of existence.

◆

Dear Barry

I am a thirty-two year old businessman. All through my life, there has been a feeling inside me of there being a bigger purpose in life than just working and being married. I could never figure out what: another job, another wife, hobby? I divorced my wife three years ago. It killed me but I knew I had to do it, although I didn't know why. I also knew that I had to straighten out my life before I could ever really be happy.

In my search for what to do and how to do it, I had relationships with two beautiful women. I loved them very much but inside me was the feeling I had to face myself first.

Shortly after, I heard one of your tapes. Your teaching has given me tremendous clarity about life, my self and Me. It became relatively easy to straighten out my life because I'm used to taking responsibility for things in my work — but my self is the hardest thing to take responsibility for. There were two difficult areas: my coping with woman and letting go of the personality. I have done it. I now see woman in all her beauty and mystery, without expectation about love or sex. She is no more a reflection of my sexuality, she is beautiful and she is my love.

I feel more a man than ever before because I can love her honestly and give without the need for anything from her. It comes naturally. And woman recognises it in all her beauty.

In my 'shallow' existence as a businessman there was hotel life, new people every day and much aloneness. I find that I give much more now and therefore feel so much better that finally I have started to truly love life, my work and all people. In love I am able to forgive them for anything they do to me in the moment. (It almost sounds religious, but it's not.)

This tremendous feeling of peace inside me is beautiful. I realise with my whole being that this was 'the greater purpose' in life that I have felt in me all my life. I feel great gratitude, first of all to the realisation of love and life, the Most High; and secondly, to the man who reflected it to me with such clarity and authority that I was able to find peace inside me so fast. I know that I am only just starting to realise, but for some reason I am in peace all the time lately. I'm sure it never stops, it is impossible to stop. But that's not important: it's the beauty of it that is important to me.

I thank the God inside me every day.

Mark

Mark

Thank you for writing. There is nothing like gratitude and love of the Most High to make a man of man.

I trust that all continues to be well with you. At thirty-two there is still much life to be lived and it is a wonderful thing that you go into that space at such a young age with the realisations of love and truth you reveal in your letter.

There are no reasons — just life. Life is peace and reasons have reason to be troubled.

◆

*True love in the family is when
someone reveals to the members
where they are being dishonest
to God or truth.*

Dear Barry Long

I am twenty-four and am endeavouring to live the divine life to the best of my ability. I'm facing a crisis and don't know what to do. I've been with my partner Heather for five months now, making love according to your teaching and trying to put honesty first.

Heather has now put it all on the line by saying that I must be prepared to have children with her; otherwise I don't love her. She already has a son by a previous lover. I feel it would destroy our love to have a child (or children) now: it takes so much energy to be straight that our love would suffer and the child would suffer.

I see it as a big responsibility to raise a child (twenty years) and I don't feel quite ready for that. It doesn't feel right to give her a child just because she wants one. What about my *responsibility for the child?*

This might be a case of dying for love, dying to my position of not wanting responsibility for a child. I don't know. Shouldn't it feel 'right' to die for love?

Heather says that I don't know what love is if I'm not prepared to have children, that I don't know how to love her. Man doesn't know what love is — only woman does. So what's the truth here?

Joshua

Joshua

Regarding your problem: I am speaking to you now, to no other man or woman. You must do what you feel is right for you. You must not follow what anybody else says or has said. You must be true to yourself in this crisis, as you call it. If you are not, you will be unable to be true to the situation of what man is with woman; you will have conflict as you have now and from that place will be unable to love her rightly; you will put your emotional tension out on others; and you will have endless questions arising in you as your letter shows.

But, to be true to yourself rightly in this situation and take the course which is opposed to your partner's desire, you must be prepared for her to leave you. You must, in other words, die for what you feel is right for you if that's how it has to be. You must not complain or be regretful afterwards. You must accept willingly, like a man, the adjudication of life for the price of you taking responsibility for what you feel is right for you. That is dying for what is right and that is the same as dying for love or truth. If it is right you will feel right in what you have done, in not compromising. The key is, I must die for what I feel is right — otherwise it is likely to be just another want. In other words, I must be prepared to lose all — and stick to it without backsliding.

Incidentally true love is the love of God and truth, not the love of children or any other object. A woman cannot love the man first, let alone her child. To be true she must love the God within her first and then she will know what true love is in the world. Man and woman only make children for the perpetuation of existence. Their real purpose is to make true love so that it removes the attachment to existence from both of them. To love one another truly reveals the God in each; then only the absent consciousness of the unknown remains.

◆

Dear Barry

*After many years of not being able to see my children, I asked
you how I should deal with the situation. You suggested that
I continue to acknowledge them. This seemed right and
true to me. Miraculously, that same Christmas time, my
children contacted me again. Since then they have visited
me and my son Ben has been with me several times.*

*I've seen that Ben carries a lot of disturbance in his
psyche and much unresolved hurt, anxiety and pain. Still,
it seemed that during our time together something sweet
and precious also came to the surface: the pain began to
be converted to love.*

*Ben has now become very ill and he and his mother
have asked if it would be possible for him to come and live
with my partner, Joanna, and me for a while. We have
looked at the situation and said 'yes'. I love my son and
Joanna also loves him very much. I know from inside that
I actually have no choice in the matter. It just is that way.
I wrote and told him how Joanna and I are endeavouring
to live without unhappiness, something he and I have
already discussed during our visits, and invited him to
live in this way with us.*

*Since then Ben has expressed many fears about
coming, as has his mother. As of today, I do not know
whether it will actually happen or not, nor do I really
understand the acuteness of his physical condition. I have
no idea of the consequences for my life except that it will
probably bring major changes.*

*It seems to me that Ben's illness is related to his feel-
ing of not being loved sufficiently. Although I know my*

responsibility in the situation, I am no longer burdened by guilt in the matter. I do feel a lot of sadness and sorrow rising from my psyche, but I feel I am able to see it for what it is and not identify with it. I also know without any doubt that I love my son and that he loves me.

I have heard you say that people who are with your teaching no longer need therapy. I certainly feel that to be the truth in my life, as far as I am concerned. I also hear you say that everything in the pyramid of existence serves something below it and understand that to mean that there is a place for therapy in certain situations. I wonder whether therapy could help Ben's recovery.

How do I live simultaneously true to both the situation of living the divine life as I endeavour to do it with Joanna, and include my son and his situation which may require lengthy therapeutic or medical intervention?

Sam

Sam

First, it is imperative that you and Joanna agree to take on the Ben situation together. This is asking more of her than of you but it will not work unless she is with you all the way. It will be an action of service to the unknown or Most High on her part. And, being the man you are, you will appreciate her giving which will help to seal rightly your partnership together.

You must not allow your consideration of Ben to come between you and Joanna while you live together. Unilateral decisions must be avoided; you decide together what is best for the situation each time and agree. You are then partners.

Ben's coming may or may not eventuate. As you know, it is folly to speculate on details of what will happen when he arrives. Don't. Therapy may be necessary but that course will unfold after his arrival. First, he arrives physically and that sets everything in motion. Perhaps his arrival and simply being with you will be a major contribution to a change.

For yourself I suggest that you accept totally his coming and living with you, if he comes. It's not going to be forever. But however long, you must be prepared to go all the way until it ends — as end it surely will. The mind's compulsion is to put time on everything, to look for conclusions. When the truth is that living is a constant series of events that go on and on until death, with some events lasting longer than others but few lasting all the time. I often say I have had about five lives so far since I was born. This is true also for you. And this stage is just another life or part of the current one.

Regarding Ben, by continuing your contact with him and as a result of his visits, you have established a communication in love at the subconscious level. This is very important to what has to be done and must be deepened without any sense of trying. The boy is deeply hurt from the past and needs to know, and then to be convinced at a deep psychological level, that he is loved — and loved by you. Part of his pain is probably deep resentment against you for not having been there, for parting from his mother or from her negative input about you to him.

It is essential that from a place of love and quietude (and not from an armchair on the opposite side of the desk from his couch) that you lead him over the weeks and months to say what he is feeling. He has to be led gently down into the deeper recesses of his pain where ultimately he confides to you his terrible resentments and anger without the need to necessarily emotionalise them, although tears and sobbing are sure to come when he hits these points. You must not attempt to defend yourself in these moments nor identify with his pain. The important thing is for him to be able to say it, communicate it to you so that the river that has been dammed can flow free with the natural joy of youth, secure in the feeling of the love and wisdom of his dad.

◆

Dear Barry

I have followed your teaching for some years now and have benefited greatly from it. In this household it seems to be somewhat of a double-edged sword. My interest in your teaching has generated anger in my wife. My children who are aware of this, and confused by the negative response, tend to shy away from anything they think may be part of your teaching. The trouble is, over time I have fallen into the trap of regarding this as normal.

My question to you is: does your teaching tend to create this sort of polarisation in families, or is it a rare occurrence in your experience?

Christopher

Christopher

Unless both partners are interested or open to the teaching there is an inevitable polarisation, as you describe. If you love the teaching and find it to be the truth in your experience (as do so many thousands of others around the world), and your wife opposes it, or cannot pause to honestly see whether it's the truth in her experience, it will come between you.

I suggest you do all you can, not to force the teaching on your wife, but to sit her down and ask her please to listen to excerpts from my books and tapes and see whether, in her own experience, they are true. To do this she must put aside her conditioned thinking and reactions.

If she can show that it's not the truth, then that's fair enough, isn't it? But if she can't, then I am sure she and the children will be real enough to understand your interest without necessarily embracing it themselves.

◆

Barry

By God's grace I have been given the opportunity to go into love with a woman who lives your teaching. This is taking everything in me and I have died to much that was not right in my life. I love it, Barry, and I am changing deeply through this love and my woman's straight and true reflection.

I have been a family man for many years with children who are now adult and I'm facing all that is not right in this situation. As I get freer of the past I see the weight of expectation and familiarity in my children and ex-wife. I know this is a result of a lack of truth in me and them over the years. I find at times it is really difficult to stand against the emotional reactions that arise when I am not willing to be who I was; there is such familiarity that I often get drawn back in. There is a wrongness in what passes for love in my family and while I have indulged in this in the past, I can't live with it now. Often when I attempt to communicate truly about the love in me and the changes that are happening, I feel fear and I may get a habitual, joking response.

How can I be really true in these circumstances?

Joseph

Joseph

As you say, you have brought this on yourself; or your self has brought it on you. The problem with families is there is not enough truth between the members, as you are learning. The family of today is fundamentally dishonest, which means each one lives a relatively independent life except that each expects to be looked after according to their false notions of love. The family's notions of love are self-indulgent, self-serving, selfish.

True love in the family begins when someone, or one of their number, reveals to them their continuous emotionality — which is what you are doing. They become so used to being indulged by the indulgent father, in your case, that if he ever stops indulging them they feel he has deserted them or is denying them his love. His love, however, is to point out to each of the family when they are being dishonest, not true to God or truth, when they are demanding, expecting or familiar.

To be really true, as you yearn to be, you will have to detach yourself completely from your family. That means that you are no longer a soft touch because you are their father or their ex-husband; that you no longer give anything to your children unless they give back in doing chores around the house and rising above their emotional negativity while they are with you.

It's a war of attrition with your self. In the moment you have to stop relating as you once did. Stop feeding the family's old expectations of you. Withdraw into the fact — not into your feelings or fear.

If you are living with people who want to make fun of you while you are being straight, then sooner or later you will have to get out. They are not yet ready to listen, they haven't suffered enough to want to hear the truth.

◆

Dear Barry Long

I would be very grateful to hear your views on suicide. My wife has a number of medical problems which are causing her great distress.

Her illness is increasingly debilitating and she is now in considerable pain. She can no longer undertake the walks in the country which we used to enjoy so much. All this is depressing for her, so much so that she has written to the Voluntary Euthanasia Society for information.

As a young man before the war, I read many books on occultism and mysticism. I gained the view then that suicide was not so much wrong as pointless, since if one's karma involved suffering, this could not be avoided and suicide would merely postpone the suffering, not avoid it.

I love my wife very much and will redouble my efforts to help her. Your views would help me give her right advice.

Arthur

Arthur

The plight of your dear wife is most distressing.

But first I must assure you that suicide is neither wrong nor pointless. I cannot, and do not by any action, postpone my suffering. My life is as it is, as it unfolds moment to moment. I cannot 'take' my own life any more than I can give my life or decide when I am born. All such concepts, including that of karma, require a person, a conceiver, a doer, a decider, a believer; in other words an 'I'. The person we think we are is not real, so there is no person really to make the decision to kill herself in your beloved wife. If death happens, it happens; if life happens, it happens; there is no rational reason for either. But this, of course, is an unacceptable truth in the world of persons and five thousand million 'I's.

The virtue of life and death is beyond reasonable or personal perception or understanding. The virtue of it all is love. You love your woman. That is enough. That is pure action beyond any explaining or understanding. The integrity of life is *your* life: there is no other. And the love you have found in your life is your life's virtue. That woman is the reflection of your love, your life's virtue. The love is real; the distress and pain is not, for it will end in time. Love is out of time. And I tell you now that when this woman you love dies, you will perceive within that your love lives on in there, as long as the person, I, do not grieve for the pained form that has gone. Grieving only disturbs the field in which this extraordinary thing happens.

◆

Dear Barry Long

I am a sixty-five year old German man, a mathematics teacher, and have been practising Transcendental Meditation since 1967. I listened to you in Hamburg last year. I liked what you said very much and felt that you told the truth about life.

I have a problem and I think you are the only one who can help me to solve it. My wife has Alzheimers disease and is in a very bad condition.

I've been in a state of great anguish and have become sick. I understand the root of this is my thinking — because I am very sad at the moment. I have nobody to discuss my situation with. Could you advise me what I should do to survive this situation?

Thank you very much for everything you have already taught me in your books and tapes. I have never heard anything like this before.

Fredrik

Fredrik

You are sad at this time because you are not facing life as it is. Facing life as it is is the most difficult thing to do in the world. But it has to be done. And you will notice that practising Transcendental Meditation offers no solution to this fundamental spiritual/human problem. If TM worked you would not be writing to me. The realisation of this is also facing life as it is.

Your problem is this. Your wife has Alzheimers disease badly and there is nothing you can do about it. It would seem, on the few facts you have given me, that you either have to look after her to the end, or institutionalise her. If you look after her to the end this must be done in love. And if it is done in love you will not feel sick or anguished. For love serves and in serving is fulfilled.

If you institutionalise her this must also be done in love, a different aspect of the diamond of love. Love does not look back. Love does what is necessary because it sees what must be done for the good of all. And so if you institutionalise your wife, you must not be guilty about it, feel you have failed or feel you are unloving in doing so. Those reactions would be lack of love. You institutionalise her because it is best for her and best for you. Best for you means you will not be sorrowful in this action. You will feel a distinct release of the contraction of the anguish and sadness. And you will not radiate your unhappiness to others and therefore make the world a still more unhappy place.

Everybody has to die. There is a destructive notion, spread by unloving religions, that we all should be able to love enough to look after a spouse or close family member to the end. But the truth is each of us can only love as much as we do. To try to love and serve a notion is to fail to serve the being. I am then being true to a notion and not to love, not to what I am. I am what I am. That's life as it is, for I am life.

So get on with your life, Fredrik, and be true to what you are, not to what you think you are, what you want to be, or what others try to make you.

PS It is interesting to me that you are a teacher of mathematics. The truth is that mathematics is logical but the men and women who teach it or use it are not. The men and women are rational and therefore they are unhappy. Rational puts second thing first whereas logic puts first thing first. If you were as logical as your mathematics you would see what must be done first. Please examine what I have just said.

A year later he wrote again to Barry

Dear Mr Long

My wife is dead now and I have survived but it has been a tough time, not only for my wife but for me too. I thought many times that we, my wife and I, would both die. But it didn't happen. I am still alive. I can't tell you about everything that happened but I think you will understand.

I am now retired. After what has happened during these past few years, I have changed my opinion about life. I still like TM very much. But now, after I have read your books and listened to your tapes, I have changed my whole life totally. I want to go back through my self to Me in order to let the monster of self die and live more worthily. I cannot return to my old way of living but have already encountered many problems in facing my self.

Would it be possible for me to come to you for a few months so that I can change my life under your guidance?

Fredrik

Fredrik

Yes, as you say, after all that has happened to you, including your wife's death, 'I am still alive'. That is the truth and the end of all anxiety, once it is realised. No matter what happens I'm always 'still alive or still being'. Even when my body dies, I still am.

You are sixty-six and like the writer are preparing for death by purging yourself of the old. If TM were the truth you would have realised what I have said above by now. So TM must go. Your fear of death must go. All your thoughts about the travail you have been through must go. And as you say the monster must go, for the monster only consists of all that past I've been holding on to which is my self.

It is pleasing to hear you say you will not live that way any more. But there is no point in coming out here in the hope of being with me. You have to do it where you are. And apart from that, I do not take on students. Everyone just comes to my meetings. There is no personal instruction.

If you're really serious come and be with me at my meetings as often as you can. My personal presence is more penetrating than my books and tapes. This will give you the energy you need to change your life.

I acknowledge that you are earnest in your resolve.

◆

LOVE

*Every woman is like you. She too
is waiting for someone she can
love who will love her.*

Dear Barry

I am twenty-eight years old and have been practising your teaching for seven years. All my life all I've ever wanted to do is love a woman, but the opportunity has never been given to me, except for a short time when I was nineteen. You say the right person will be drawn to you in time, but I feel she will never come. Surely I have waited long enough? I cannot by decision or choice, go out to find a woman because this doesn't work. Must not the opportunity be given by life, even for me to act on it?

Thank you very much.

John

John

I suspect that now you have written to me as you have, a woman will appear in the next few days or weeks for you to love. She may even be in your circle of acquaintances now. The point is you may not have noticed her. You may be looking for some sort of ideal — your image of the woman you want. *That* woman is not going to come.

Seven years without an opportunity suggests to me that the above is the case; or that you are afraid to approach a woman (perhaps because she may decline and you don't want to feel foolish); or you simply make excuses to yourself for not responding when the opportunity is there.

First. You must feel in yourself where a woman is attracted to you. There will be indications in her speech and manner — all very subtle, pleasant. She may not be a beauty — but are you, or am I? It is woman you want to love and the beauty a man needs is certainly not in the skin. It's in the flesh, inside. Respond. Give. Be honest. Time and association tell. The deepest love is frequently that which starts where you never suspected it.

Second. You must be brave, by being simple and overcoming the inevitable lack of confidence that has really kept you from her.

Don't try to be anything you may have read. Don't copy another man. Be John. Trust in what God made you. Go up to her. Open your mouth. And say in a gentle but straight way why you are speaking to her. You liked the way she smiled. You enjoy her cheery manner. Or her directness.

Third. Every woman is like you. She too is waiting for someone to love and to love her. She has been taught and learned to be wary. And she, too, often lacks self-confidence — which she may cover up with an appearance of being cold, disinterested or even flippant and flighty. Just say it as it is, as you are. No need for clever personality. What you are is best. But make sure you don't give her your unhappiness.

Fourth. You have to court a woman. Quick fixes are the order of the times — but they soon come apart with little but pain and disillusionment being achieved. Set out to win her. Do this first by setting out to win every woman you talk to — the next old lady even, that you happen to talk to. Every woman has something if you give her the time and the recognition of what you see as you address her. Tell her, even if it's acknowledging her courage in walking up the street with her heavy shopping bag — which you may ask if you could help her with. Give of yourself to every woman and you will never be short of the love of woman.

Fifth. Ask yourself, is this man Barry Long silly or impractical or a bit mad? Or could it be that he is telling you at twenty-eight the secret of his long life of how to really love woman and to win her love?

Sixth. There is only one woman, man. And she is listening and watching in every woman. She is immortal, timeless. She has all the time in the world as she waits for man to discover in the flesh that inasmuch as he sees and acknowledges some aspect of her in every female form he addresses, she comes to him as his heart's desire manifest.

◆

Barry

I am thirty years old and have made love to one woman (for a few months) and, apart from being with a prostitute when I was a young man, I have no other experience of woman. I now want to know the absolute truth of woman and my place with her as I am dying inside.

When I see her, I am absolutely in awe of her beauty. I go still and I see her and can't take my eyes off her beauty. She knows this: she often approaches me as she knows that I love her. I am aware that my love of her brings a joy into her face. This happens frequently with any woman I happen to notice, wherever or whoever she may be.

Then, when she speaks to me, it seems that this just isn't her talking. This isn't love talking: it is something speaking through her. It is as though her words are apart from the beauty I see. I can't listen to her without losing touch with this beauty. To me, love and beauty are still. That's why I listen to your tapes so much, Barry, because I know you know that too.

When I speak to woman, it isn't me talking either. My words are utterly separate from the love I see. I talk rubbish and often find myself criticising her in some way as an automatic reaction. Is it true that conversation is utterly superficial and an escape from love? But if I don't talk, women leave, probably thinking I'm not interested.

I suffer from great feelings of inadequacy and self-doubt. My emotionally distant father drummed into me that I was an idiot and I spent my teenage years feeling utterly inferior. I am well below average height and am deeply hurt by the prejudice of people concerning my height. I am particularly conscious of my height when with woman.

I would welcome any guidance on how to approach a woman right from the start, or what to do if a woman approaches me. This is an area of enormous difficulty as I know my fear and lack of experience make me appear hopelessly inadequate.

The possibility of a woman agreeing to see me again brings up several fears: that I will have to perform in some way to please her, that she will see through me and see that I am empty, that I am nothing.

The problem is, how can I be true to woman and be the stillness? She doesn't want to know about stillness in my limited experience. All the men are talking about being someone, or doing something, or creating something. And I am nothing. I know that's the truth. But I have a desire to love woman, to make love with her and unite myself in my body. How can I do this and make her interested in me? It seems to me that to attract a woman, a man must lie. Everybody seems to be living a lie and speaking lies to each other. I have to be true.

I feel the answer is to stay with the love of woman within me. But as soon as she appears outside me, I just don't know what to do. What does woman want? What does she want to hear from me so that we can make love together?

Thomas

Thomas

What does this woman that you love want? She wants you to be exactly what you are. You must be true to that to be true to her. What are you?

You are short. You have wonderful still grey eyes. Your face is sensitive, good to look at and its expression straight. You truly do love the Woman behind women. She — that great intelligence that when realised fully is exclaimed to be God or living love — knows this.

You must not endeavour to impress, persuade, convince or perform in any other way than what you naturally are. This, even if it takes a lifetime.

But it won't.

Your error is in trying to be what you are not, in trying to fulfil the expectations of women and your own conditioned mind's expectations of what is required for you to attract woman. This makes you fearful and uncertain.

When you meet a woman who attracts you, you must address her from the place of your attraction within you and inform her precisely of what is happening there. You must not consider what you are going to say for that would destroy the honesty and spontaneity of your divine attraction and recognition of the woman you are seeing in that form.

I would not say that to an ordinary man, that is to a man who is overtly on the prowl sexually, the predator who has conditioned women to mistake dishonesty, personality and sophistication for incipient love or sincere attraction.

But you are different. Are you hearing me, Thomas? I said you are different. You truly love the divine woman in the form and so, for instance, when you speak directly from that place of recognition as I have suggested above, it is natural to say to the woman such things as, 'I find you very beautiful. I enjoy the way you smile at people. You have joy in your eyes which shows me that you love life. I am attracted to you and it is a pleasure to speak to you as I am now for I too love life. And I enjoy acknowledging beauty and simplicity when I see it. I don't ask you to say anything in return but I just wanted to tell you that.'

Such statements, when they come from the place you have inside of you, will be heard by the woman behind the conditioning. If her conditioning is still too heavy she will respond in some distractive or trite way and you will just have to nod your head and say, 'That's okay. I meant it but I don't expect anything from you'. But, if she's a woman she'll respond somehow from that place. You may have a lot of failures but who cares: she wants you to learn to accept yourself as you are.

Your self-doubt is utterly unacceptable to me and to the Woman that you love. Whether she is attracted to you or not is of no consequence. The law is that if you are attracted to her, then the potential is there for her to be attracted to you, provided you speak from the place of your attraction. If you speak from your head you will speak from self-doubt or fear — the personality that your background induced you to develop to cover your pain and insecurity. When you speak from the place of attraction you bypass the personality and your straightness, your clear grey eyes and expression will communicate the openness and sincerity that you are.

One step at a time. Speak from the honesty of your attraction first. The coming together and the making of love will follow as you stay true to what you are. If she responds, remember you will have to woo her. That means that if you enjoy being with her that you tell her so and endeavour to be with her without necessarily trying to make love to her until that is demonstrated to be right by the attraction. Wooing her still means being honest to your attraction to her. Woman will do the rest. But do not be discouraged by failure or rejection by women. They won't be able to go into the mystery of love with you which is what you truly desire.

Woman — the woman — will test you, man. The feeling of rejection is a selfish feeling, a consideration of self. And in love there can be no self-consideration. Self is only your *notion* or impression of what you are and what is expected of you. It is not the truth. The truth is that you love woman as you described to me in your letter and you are true to that love, that place inside of you. Be honest to that, Thomas, and you will be honest to woman and she will love you. But you must not love your self.

I am looking for man willing to die for love (die to himself as I have explained in this letter) so that woman will have a man worthy to die for.

◆

Dear Barry

I told you at the last Gold Coast meeting that I was afraid of woman. It would be more true to say that I'm afraid of love, to be love. I see now that all *my fears are sex based: all my fears around women are due to the guilt engendered by the realisation that I have put sex into her.*

All my restlessness comes from this social-psychological fear that keeps me from being true, honest, courageous, innocent and loving. I also feel woman's fear of the sex in me and my subsequent shame. All woman wants to see in me is that life is good and it's good to be alive. They mostly see the world in me and the lack of ease I convey.

How can I surrender this worldliness, Barry? I'm seeing that I'm living purposelessly and don't have sufficient courage to live more wisely and rightly — although the greater part of me is really wanting to stop suffering.

Nick

Nick

First, you have done well in writing as you have about your fear of love. The seeing of that and all that you wrote is part of the solution you are seeking.

Second, you ask what you can do to live more rightly and wisely. The answer is, love woman. Accept every opportunity to communicate to her your knowledge that 'life is good and it's good to be alive' (your words). Live what you've realised and said, Nick. Don't allow self-doubt to make you feel ill at ease. Give her your sweet nature when you speak to her or meet her. This is not an act of personality for you have realised, and written (exposed) to me, what she wants to see. So do it.

That will stop the suffering as you persevere and cross the barrier of fear by doing.

◆

Dear Mr Long

Since the age of twenty-three or so, I have suffered several nervous breakdowns. I feel I'm breaking down now. I find myself struggling all the time on my own and in the dark, against I know not what. I have been to psychiatrists and spiritual healers but always felt that somehow they didn't know what I was talking about.

I have never had a love affair nor made love. I am a thirty-five year old heterosexual.

I am putting into effect all you say on your tapes but it feels too late. I know it's all my fault but I did the best I could and I am not giving up.

Trevor

Trevor

You write clearly and you are doing your best. You must give up feeling 'it is your fault'. The key to opening up your psyche is for you to know the love and physical presence of woman.

Obviously, this is not easy for you, otherwise you would have done something about it after all these years. But that does not alter the fact that unless a man has had the physical love of woman, and possesses a sensitivity of spirit which I sense in you, he will feel something radical is missing. The love of woman is essential to man's existence as a complete being. Having 'missed out' on that, that shadow of the absence of the fundamental experience of love will tend to disturb you psychically. The solution for you is to overcome your diffidence and to begin with start speaking to woman about the love and truth you know. Unless you take action you are going to continue to drift in this limbo. It is your fear of facing woman, your self-consciousness and self-doubt that is the barrier.

◆

Dear Barry

I have written several letters to you during the last six years with questions regarding what, at the time, I regarded as the main obstacles to my being in Me. I now find that the problem I am not facing and have not asked you about is one which, if truly faced, will demand great responsibility of me.

I am an actor and at present am a member of one of the major Shakespearean theatre companies in England. For twenty years I have suffered from acute stage-fright, have tried every available 'treatment' and now drink a quantity of whisky whenever I appear on stage in a principal part. I realise I have an investment in this fear and in looking at it, can see that it proves to me my deep-lying belief that I am worthless, repulsive and worthy of people's scorn.

To be true, the dichotomy which appeared to confound me has been:

a) Facing the fact that my job makes me unhappy and in order to find peace (or relief) I must move on to some occupation where there was not the same strain.

b) In doing that I would not be facing the fear and it would recur in another form.

I know that there is truth in this and having looked at it for some years, cannot see it by myself.

Can you help me?

Timothy

Timothy

You must first face the fact that you are afraid of woman, afraid to truly love her, afraid to cross the line and be available to her. That is the core of your problem. Your 'treatments' have been an avoidance and the whisky, as you know, is a temporary uplifting and the inevitable down-going of the wrong love.

Acting is a compatible love, compatible with the woman you can love. Your job is not the problem. You are serving the people there. Here again, in the symbol of your life, the audience (quite rightly) represents your love and you perform splendidly for her, giving her much pleasure. But it is a pleasure you do not receive (on the surface) because you refuse to love her and therefore feel 'exposed' when you have to display your undeniable love and sensitivity through your natural creativity as an actor.

Woman, the poetry, the muse, the communication of love, loves you and admires you — if only you will be what you are and act for her with all the gusto and sweetness of complete giving.

Now get on with it, Timothy. Overcome your fear of her by doing, not thinking. A woman you are attracted to is there somewhere, or she will be, after you digest what I've said. Start with conversation about acting if you will; but get to the point and the point is love. And love physically as soon as you can and take her on — even though your precious independence or fear writhes at the prospect of being true to love or woman.

Two years later he wrote again.

Dear Barry

When I wrote to you a couple of years ago about stage fright, you replied that I was not loving woman rightly. I saw the truth of that and began to live it.

A short time ago I 'discovered' (uncovered) Woman in the body of my wife of thirty years. It is glorious. I wanted to tell you and thank you.

◆

Barry

I am alone and experience great loneliness and an intense longing to love woman. Sometimes I can observe the pain and longing in a detached way. But at other times I get angry and shout at God. It happened again this morning. Then I realised that my love of God is real and this calmed me down. I have decided that rather than torture myself by longing for woman, I will simply enjoy my love of God.

Stephen

Stephen

Yes, love God. That's all you can do, and all you need to do, until your life changes and you have the opportunity to love woman. The love of woman, for man, is the love of God in existence. God is out of existence, beyond existence and the task for all of us is to bring that indefinable principle into existence. The swiftest way is to love woman, not to get rid of my anger, not to get something for myself, not to find God, but simply to love her because I love her. This is not personal, just as the love of God is not personal. In other words there is no single form for God and there is no single form for woman. God in woman is where she appears for you in your life and the task then is simply to love her for the principle, not the form that she is.

◆

*You may love your woman but
do you love her enough?*

Dear Barry

I have never been exposed to your teaching before. I am a divorced man in my fifties who is having the most disturbing experience of my life. It all flows from my meeting and becoming totally overwhelmed by a woman, Rose, who lives your teaching.

I cannot explain why I am so completely attracted to Rose although I know part of it is to do with the aura of serenity that surrounds her, plus her unfailing cheerfulness in all circumstances. She rarely stops smiling!

I want desperately to enter into a permanent, committed relationship with her. Unfortunately however, although she displays a caring and loving attitude towards me, she will not consider such a relationship until such time as I look at 'the pain of the past that lives inside me'. I am happy to do this guided by her, but seek reassurance that she will still be there for me when 'I dissolve the pain'. She refuses point blank to give such a reassurance saying that neither of us can put 'a noose around love', although I feel I have no difficulty in doing so.

The pain that Rose's attitude causes me is enormous, reducing me to tearful confusion — a state that has been totally unfamiliar to me in my life so far. It is extremely distressing.

I feel completely at ease and enjoy being with Rose. Yet I've only known her a few weeks. Being with her is a unique and beautiful experience. However the things she says to me totally 'blow my mind' and I feel I am being turned both upside down and inside out simultaneously!

I kiss and fondle her naked body in bed in accordance with strict parameters set by her. Obviously at some stage I will want to make love with her and whilst there is no desperate urgency, I have said as much to her. However, her reply is always the same: she won't make love to 'an emotional man' and one who has an all-consuming 'attachment' to her.

I have asked why, given her blank refusal to move our relationship forward from where it is now, she remains with me. Her reply is that 'she sees in me a very loving, non-sexual man'. She is prepared to assist, guide and help me in any way she can to enable me 'to dissolve the pain of the past'.

I want (and will do anything) to make our love work in the way Rose describes but am totally nonplussed by her refusal to commit herself in any way to me when 'I dissolve the pain of my past'.

Given my sincerity and utter bewilderment, Rose has suggested that I write to you as she knows you are 'more powerful and energetic' than she is and will assuredly 'have the key to my dilemmas'. I accept this because I love her and have total confidence in what she tells me.

I sincerely want to spend the rest of my life with Rose. Please give me guidance on how to achieve my wishes. I'll read, listen to and do anything that will enable me to be on a level plane with her and reach some mutual understanding.

Ray

Ray

It is you who must move the relationship forward, not Rose. She is willing if you will only do your part. And your part involves getting rid of the pain of the past that lives in you. What is this past that you are holding on to? What is it that you love more than Rose, although you protest that you love her most? Do you love some guilt arising from your actions in the past? Or is it the love of the pain of not having been able to love in the past, or be loved? Whatever it is you are not being responsible for your love now and that's what Rose is trying to convey to you. How can a woman love you if you love your own pain of the past more than her? Please look at this question and be practical and sensible as you do so. Would you want to love a woman who loved her pain more than you? Rose's 'unfailing cheerfulness' which you speak of is because she has given up her love of past pain.

Another area in which you are in error is that you keep asking her for a commitment. This also is because of your past pain which makes you too insecure to accept love that is demonstrated every moment and therefore does not need a commitment. You would bring love down to the ordinary level where most people love and live and Rose is not going to surrender to that. You say you are being turned both upside down and inside out. Well, would you expect to love a woman like Rose if you were the same man as you have been in your life up to now, who did not understand that he himself is responsible for his freedom from pain and unhappiness? You are in love and it sounds to me that love is doing a first class job on you.

The attachment Rose speaks of is not actually your attachment to her but your attachment to your own pain which is the source of your doubts and fears. What she is saying (and of course I have not spoken to her) is that when you give up your emotional pain you will discover that you love her and there will be no more demands from you for some sort of promised security which does not exist in this life. You may die tonight or she may die tonight, apart from the other movements of life; so how can you in truth speak of a commitment that binds?

◆

Dear Barry

I am married to a beautiful, courageous, loving and very spiritual woman, Catherine. I love the beauty in her but I am not worthy of her. I know that the same selfless love I see in her resides deeply in me too but I am not able to manifest or communicate it. Instead I often find myself feeling resentful towards her, acting selfishly and sometimes even being quite spiteful. This causes her and me great pain, although she gets around it and continues to give to me and love me in a truly remarkable fashion. The more beautiful she becomes the more I seem to try and hurt her. I can't understand why I need to undermine her but it happens in spite of me.

As I write this I am feeling an intense pain in my solar plexus and the tears are flowing. I do not wish to hurt my love.

Barry, please help.

Brad

Brad

You have a mother problem and you'd better deal with it or you'll lose her.

The intense feeling of pain in your solar plexus, as you wrote, is it. You were not loved by your mother or she could not give you the love you craved. Also, your father may have resented or hated her. The pained little boy in you — he's still in there weeping as a deep emotion —

admires Catherine, looks to her for love but knows that no matter what, it's not going to be forthcoming. So her actions of love, though observed by the man you are now, are construed through the unhappy child emotion of unrequited love of the mother.

Then the resentment comes, the selfish 'what about me, my pain?' and with it the hurtful need to spoil, to injure, to punish meanly, nastily and pettily. There is a certain adultness in this as well. Are you by any chance still harbouring resentment you had as a young man against a former lover you tried to treat as Mum which made her turn against you? As you say, you're doing it. You from the past.

It's time to stop.

First, know that I know you have the same selfless love inside of you. That is the truth. You must acknowledge this continually, when it is there, without ifs or buts. First thing first.

Then you have to rid yourself of this pained and crying boy. He lies kicking his feet and thumping his hands on top of the selfless love you are. When you try to express the love towards your woman, or to be that love in existence, it comes out through the boy, distorted and pernicious.

Go and see Mum (and then Dad if necessary) as you must have heard me describe so often at my meetings. Tell her of the boy's pain; how she did her best for you for which you thank her gratefully and lovingly; how you the man don't blame her in any way or hold anything against her; how you love her (if you do) and how you just needed to say this for yourself, to free yourself of your own childish misunderstanding of love.

Only such practical action will do the job. And give up thinking you're unworthy if you do. That's the child, too, the emotion sucking pathetically off you. There is no room in this for guilt, remorse or sorrow. They are self, not selfless. Be the man I know you are.

Go back out there and face yourself as I have described. Until you do, you won't be able to look your love in the eye, inside or out.

◆

Dear Barry

There are several areas in my life I would like to ask you about.

I feel guilty for all sorts of reasons: for wanting to listen to your tapes instead of being with my wife who's not 'into' your teaching; for wanting to listen to music tapes instead of your tapes; for not meditating; for missing out on an exercise activity (I have difficulty choosing between activity and the inactivity of being in Me). What can I do about this?

I am disturbed by my wife's smoking habit. Despite my concern for her health and constant nagging about a habit that is offensive to me, she will not stop. How can we resolve our difference of opinion about this? I do love her but this issue drives a wedge between us.

We are infrequent lovers, but when we do make love it is very nice and we both enjoy it. As neither of us uses contraception, I have to ejaculate outside by her masturbating me after we have finished. You say the penis is not meant for the hand, so how can I get around this? I ask her to masturbate me sometimes for my release. Is this wrong or selfish of me? I never force myself on her but she doesn't seem to need release like I do: a cuddle and kiss is enough for her. Do you think this is my fault as maybe in the past I have been unkind to her and made her withdraw from me? She also dislikes oral sex so we hardly ever do it, though I would like it.

Martin

Martin

Fundamentally it seems to me your guilt complex is being fed by not being honest in your partnership. You may love your wife, and she may love you, but do you love her enough? It seems to me you both need to have a serious conversation. I suspect your guilt comes from falling in with your wife's demands in exchange for occasional sexual pleasure. Your sexuality is allowing you to be manipulated. It's time you started doing or living precisely what is right for you. You will be unable to do that, without guilt or doubt, while your sexuality manipulates you into trade-offs.

◆

Dear Barry

Since returning from the Master Session I've seen a pattern arising between my partner and I.

What happens is that a small incident sparks off an argument between us. For instance, this evening Barbara asked me to feed the cats as she was going out. That was fine and I agreed to do it. Ten minutes later she told me again that the cats were ready to be fed and that they had no food at the moment. My reaction was to become defensive, distant and cold and ask her, 'Why are you telling me again? I know I have to feed the cats.'

As I became more precise and distant, Barbara became more and more emotional, trying to explain what she had meant.

This kind of stand-off seems to continually arise between us. When I can't get a grip on the situation in the moment, she goes into a downward spiral. We eventually get out of it, but it leaves a bad taste in my mouth and baffles me. What am I doing wrong?

Jerry

Jerry

You both must get closer to the situation. Your separation from the fact and truth of the situation is where the separation starts between you at any time.

Were the cats so hungry that Barbara had to speak to you the second time because you had failed to appreciate, or she had failed to communicate, that they needed to be fed now or within a few minutes? Or, if the cats were not that hungry and you had said you were going to feed them, why did she need to tell you again? She must answer whether there was any need, or whether she was just acting out of the habit of wanting to say something habitually before going out. Or does she not trust you to feed them in a reasonable time? Does she feel that you may not feed them for another hour? Has your behaviour in the past shown that you may take your own time and not be alive to what you've undertaken to do?

Is the case that you don't listen and she tries to dominate you, one being the effect of the other?

You both ought to get to the core of it, where the first sign of disagreement, frustration, defensiveness and hostility occurs.

Anyway, why was she going out? Do you resent her leaving you alone? Does she suspect you're likely to take it out on the cats? And why, if she's so concerned didn't she feed the cats herself? What's going on between you that hasn't been said yet, let alone faced?

◆

Dear Barry Long

My reason for writing is a sore issue between my partner, Jennifer and I.

I have a close friend called Bob. We share a lot of chat about spirituality. He is a non-judgmental man and I feel he is quite spiritually mature. He is the most consistently 'happy' person I have ever met. But Jennifer dislikes him. She thinks he is 'in love' with me and that our relationship is 'unnatural'. I have confronted him about whether his feelings towards me were sexual and he has always said no. I have never felt anything like this between us.

I am sick of fighting with Jennifer over this. All I have asked is that she not speak unkindly of a good friend of mine and she has refused. I find her judgment of others unbearable at times, especially when it seems so unfounded. Is it wrong to feel spiritual love for close male friends and to value their company?

Lewis

Lewis

From what you say, Jennifer is jealous of your association with your friend. Woman will tend to do this because the female principle requires all of a man's love and cannot abide his need to love a friend. That's fine if the woman is love, for then the man she is with would have no need of such a friend. The friend may still exist but he would not be particular. Jennifer is not giving you everything you require, so you need a friend.

It is not good for anyone to judge another for it means that they are judging their self and that will make them emotional and discontented.

◆

Dear Barry Long

I have been in a relationship with a woman for fourteen years. Due to a severe illness, the past two years have been particularly trying for me and my partner's loving support and devotion seem to know no bounds. I am deeply touched and moved by this and yet I feel our relationship — as a sexual man/woman partnership — is over.

When she raises the subject of our relationship, I just talk vaguely and say I am not sure of anything at the moment while I am ill. She is so sweet and loving I would absolutely hate to hurt her— and I think it would hurt her a lot if I said I felt our relationship was over. Yet should I be honest and say what I feel to be the truth?

Carl

Carl

You must tell her what you told me, that your relationship as a sexual partnership has ended. Things have changed for you during your illness and you tell her this because you must be honest with her. The woman in her wants honesty in love more than anything else she may think she wants. Do not tell her you want to be friends with her. That is a most insulting thing to say to a woman when you are ending a sexual partnership.

No matter how deeply distressed she is, you must not back off and take pity on her; you must continue to be honest that the sexual relationship is finished and offer no hope to her in that sense for the future. You will feel fear in doing this, saying this, but that is the fearful self you must sacrifice to gain the integrity of strength on both sides which you will see arises out of such sacrifice. It must be clear and kept clear that that is how it is.

When your health returns you must not go back to her sexually (to fulfill any loneliness or when the sexual urge assails you) unless you are prepared to take her on fully once again. Then she will have the strength to get through. It is man's dishonesty with woman, his cowardly self-protection, which he justifies on the basis of not wanting to hurt her, that saps her integrity and strength when she has to face his severance of her sexual dependence on him.

◆

Dear Barry

I have a problem concerning my partner. We have been on and off for the past couple of years but have been together for about five years or so. I left her a couple of times because, to be frank, she was treating me like hell and I couldn't stand it any more.

To make a long, long, story short we are back together again and things are better than before but still not good. She complains about everything and brings up past sorrows over and over again. I try to remain calm in my endeavour to take her on but she starts from nowhere and keeps rising and rising until I cannot maintain myself any longer and I give in to her arguments.

I have asked her to listen to your tapes and read your books with me and at first she did, but with little effort on her part to stay present. She is a Catholic and attests that she is doing the right thing, which is fair enough, I never put her down for her need to do what she does. I tell her the truth because sometimes she asks for it but she makes sarcastic remarks about your teachings and calls me a cult member.

You have said that man must take on woman's karma. I'm beginning to wonder how much karma this woman has or if I am stuck on a karmic merry-go-round only to wind up where I started because I missed the signal to get off.

I want to leave, Barry, but I want to do the right thing by woman. I do not want to be selfish but I need some peace.

Andrew

Andrew

It is folly to cast your pearls in front of those who do not want them and use them as missiles. Eventually if this woman does not start to listen intelligently to what you are saying, and what you are living as the truth, you will leave her. You won't have to make a decision. It will just happen. Many people delight in being unhappy and find it impossible to live any other way. Keep loving and forgetting as best you can and the solution will be done for you.

◆

Dear Barry

At a meeting you said that all the self has to come out eventually. After some painful and sleepless nights facing my self (guilt and self-doubt), I realised that this does not mean the self has to be expressed, but has to come out of hiding so that what you called the superior faculty of pure intellect can shine on it. Does the light of intellect change the nature of that which is seeking expression or remove the need for it?

I have felt confusion about making love with my partner when it sometimes becomes wild and animal-like. Leila has helped me by giving me very clear feedback while we are making love. She says that the energy of the wild and natural animal is beautiful and she feels a lot of love and beauty; but that the minute I get excited and self-ish, I lose contact with her and the beauty. I am not as alert with it as she is, but I feel what she says to be true. Is there anything else I am failing to perceive here?

I have shame and guilt regarding my last relationship with a woman with whom I began to explore your teaching. I left her, feeling I had gathered too much past in the years we were together. Yet I feel I failed in the end to give seventy times seven chances when I left, too tired to face the fiendess further and attracted to the stillness of a fresh love. However I haven't been able to stop thinking about my previous lover, for there was a lot of love between us. You have recommended that we don't see or think of each other. Is there anything positive I can do with this yearning to continue giving? Is negation the only appropriate giving here?

Arnold

Arnold

Yes, the light of pure intellect changes the nature of that which is seeking expression — and once changed in this way the need of it does not have to be removed.

In other words, we are all born with a positive nature, the need to self project. The process and purpose of living is to render the nature negative — aligned with or surrendered to what is or the divine will. Negation of self by pure intellect, not by the mind of concepts, is the way.

Regarding your question about lovemaking. What your woman says is correct — although she does not need me to tell her that. Listen to her where love is concerned. She loves the natural animal. But detests the beast. The animal (love) is of the wild. The beast creeps into the animal — as sex — from it being caged in the mind of civilisation.

Regarding your last question about your former lover. Your honesty, or let us say your lack of resolution, has to be in question here. You cannot love two women honestly if you are with one and thinking about the other. If you long to be with the former lover you should go and be with her wholly and not think about this one.

Your question, 'Is there anything I can do about this yearning to continue giving' is a red-herring and a euphemism. You are not giving, man. You are not giving to that woman, obviously, and you're certainly not giving to the woman you're with. You're withholding from both or giving a bit of your self to each which is *not* giving.

◆

Barry

I don't know what to do about my woman's sister, Margaret. She has been very unhappy and emotional for many years and this evening even spoke on the phone about the possibility of suicide.

Last year we spoke a lot together but I don't know how to help her any more or what to say. She has had a few love affairs in the past. These didn't last long or were problematical. She hasn't had a lover for three years now, although she is longing for it.

I have thought (and still think sometimes) about loving her and taking her on as a partner. I have spoken to you about this and your advice helped me to become more clear about the situation.

But it's very difficult for me to stop thinking about her or get her out of my mind.

Graham

Graham

The question is a simple one: are you prepared and willing to die for her? If not, you won't have the power to help her; you will become restless and discontented, she will become even more emotional and hysterical and your current woman self-doubting and unhappy.

All that emotion in her, you (as her love/lover) will have to take on so you can remove it from her. She will put it on you, inevitably, for that is the process. Can you take it and dissolve it in the unshakeable presence in yourself without generating more in her, more despair, as most men do? Saving woman from her self, the shadow of the sexual world men have put into her by their ignorance and lack of love, is a job for Man, not for men. Nevertheless, this is the most noble thing man can do for his love, woman, who is entrapped in the world he built for his self.

If you take her on, she will be in two bodies. You have to take her on in both, for what you do for Margaret cannot be done at the expense of Susan. Susan too must go deeper. You must be honest to both and both must be willing to participate for love — not for self, sex or excitement.

Really to do this you have to be a tantric master*. And as you are not, I suggest you choose one woman or the other and free her of her emotions and in so doing, free yourself. Your attraction to the sister is primarily sexual, not selfless.

◆

---

* The tantric master has the God-given power to love woman physically and bring her to life, which means giving her the knowledge of a love she has not known before. This love is synonymous with the love of God.

Dear Barry

I have been with my partner, Lisa, for a year and enjoy being with her. We were very absorbed in each other for the first few months and felt a lot of energy. This hasn't changed much although we make love less often.

I also enjoy being with another woman, Maria. I feel love for her and am attracted to her as I am attracted to Lisa, which may seem strange. I have resisted making love to Maria out of a desire to be true to Lisa and to avoid causing pain to her and to myself.

There is sufficient love for me to make love with Maria. The only problem is my conscience.

Barry, could you please help me to see clearly. What is happening? Is it God or life wanting me to make love to two women and I am afraid of it — or is it sex wanting to have excitement?

David

David

It is sex wanting to have excitement — unless you can love both women so that neither they nor you become more unhappy. The chances of this are just about negligible unless you, the man, have realised love, and the women realise that you are love.

The problem to begin with, as you describe it, is that Lisa wants you to make love with her but not with Maria, for you say she would be hurt. So if you go ahead Lisa is already going to be unhappy; and that will make you unhappy. Maria will only be happy for a time, for sooner or later you'll see another woman you want to make love to as well. This will make Maria unhappy . . .

I suggest you stick with one or the other woman. It's hard enough for most men to love enough to make one woman happy, let alone two.

A finer question is, why would Lisa be hurt?

In woman's present condition, all who love a man will be hurt if he makes love to another woman. This is because all the men she has been with, including you, have not demonstrated that there is purpose in your lovemaking. You make love mostly for excitement or self-satisfaction. And woman, in the insecurity that this has caused her, makes love to assuage that insecurity and to feel for a time that she is loved. But it is a temporary solution.

Man's purpose in making love to woman is to awaken or increase her love of life or God within. In the action of making love she must know that this is happening and so must he. Otherwise the lovemaking is selfish on both parts and attachment, heartbreak or fear is sure to occur. If a woman realised that her man's love changed her by invoking a greater love of God or truth, then she would not be hurt by his making love to another woman. She would know that his love was holy and awakening as it had been for her. This may sound idealistic but then such love is an ideal and the task of man is to manifest that ideal in his own life and being.

◆

Dear Barry

Since coming to your teaching I have heard what is being said about God, love, woman, man, surrender and liberation.

What happens is until there is a reality experience in me they are just words. They are ideas, ideals, abstractions. Nothing happens until something happens in life. Then those words become reality and live.

The words 'just love', 'just love woman' seem to assume that I know what is meant and what is to be done. I do not know. I have vague notions that invariably prove to be wrong. Actually all I have are notions. My true life knowledge and experience is so thin as to be negligible. I am not daunted or disappointed. I wish to know, to live it.

I ask my woman and she speaks about love. I go to your meetings and you speak of love. I read your books and listen to your tapes.

Last night my woman questioned me. She questioned me very intelligently. We came to the essence of what it is that stops me from seeing and giving to love. I was actually able to identify my independence. To see it. Life became so simple. I looked at my independence, then turned to her. Pure, clear, simple. What had been between me and my love was gone . . . for a time. Then I could see it was between us again. It was as it had always been.

My question is: how may I surrender my independence? How may I give it up? What is the practical action please?

Carey

Carey

In that moment when you saw your independence and it left, did you see what independence in love is?

It is fear.

It is the fear of surrendering all to woman or to love. It is the fear of losing your manhood.

Independence in love is a ring of fear we surround our self with to protect our self, our fear.

In that moment of seeing your independence you saw through the fear behind it and fear, being a phantom sustained only by an ignorance, such as independence, vanished. Life became so simple (without fear). What was between you and your love (fear) was gone. But how quickly does the self as independence re-form itself under the impetus of fear.

What have you got to fear, Carey? As F D Roosevelt said, 'Only fear itself'.

How do I stop fearing?

Stop defending, stop justifying, stop asserting. Simply take a chance.

◆

Love between man and woman on this planet is invariably selfish.

Dear Barry

I'm in a very shaky state. It has been triggered by a woman I used to be with. She now lives with someone else. This didn't hurt me too much at the time. However, I met her recently and have been thrown into an emotional whirlpool. I can't sleep, I can't eat, I can hardly stop crying, my stomach is a mess and my heart is busting.

I don't want to give too much of a sad story but I feel completely helpless and raw and I can't take action. I've told her everything and she's not coming back. I've got that clear. I want to use this opportunity in the best way and I need to move on.

This has only happened twice in my thirty-nine years. The first time was ten years ago and it took over a year for the dark clouds to go. The idea of 'time slowly healing' and this continuing for any length of time is out of the question. It hurts too much. I don't want to over-indulge in it or drag it out. I just feel completely overwhelmed and I don't know what to do. I really want to move on now.

Laurie

Laurie

You must cop the pain cold turkey. But don't panic. What is happening is good. I'll tell you why and you'll know what you're doing. Keep the knowledge in front of you and you'll get through it quickly.

The two major attachments/heartbreaks in your life are wrapped up in this one current emotion. Seeing this woman triggered the mass/mess. It's not that she's not coming back — you're clear on that. It's purely the big past emotional lump rising up. It's not now; it's past — living past that is being dissolved by you simply facing it and copping the pain of yesterday's man who swept it under the carpet. It hurts. Yes. It must. But now you're mature enough, man enough, to face and dissolve the lump *consciously*. This is essential so that you can really move on. This lump has been the blockage in your life all those years. You are not to be overwhelmed. You are Laurie, my man, really doing what must be done.

You are always bigger than the problem or emotion you're facing. Just a bit perhaps, but enough. The new man is coming, behind this. Now you know, you'll be stronger.

◆

Dear Barry

What is the truth of jealousy? My lover left to go to Bali a few days ago. Before she left she told me she wished to be free to make love to other men. I didn't really know what to say, feeling she must be free to do what she wants. But since then I have been disturbed by jealous thoughts and images. I feel that I don't want to be with her if she has been with another man but is this just my emotional reaction?

Jeff

Jeff

Disaster. You love a woman who goes off to Bali on her own and before leaving tells you she wants to have the freedom to make love to other men. The cause of your jealousy is your wimpish unstraightness in putting up with such a woman in the first place. She doesn't love you enough, man. It was your hoping and euphoric way of looking at this relationship that blinded you to that simple fact.

If you love a woman do you, or any other man, want her to go and make love with other men? The answer is simply, no. So I suggest you leave her even before she arrives back; that you tell her your relationship was over the moment she left and that you will not see her or speak to her again because it is finished, over. Some men and women may not mind their lover making love with others. But that only means they don't really love them enough anyway.

When you truly love, the impulse on both sides is to spiritually consume the other, to take them into you and for you to disappear into that love forever. That is why in the 'old' days it was said that a marriage was not a marriage until it was consummated by the action of making love. It may take time to reach such a sublime realisation of love but when one or the other partner wants to go off and love others, that is intolerable to any semblance of true love.

Jealousy is the result of not seeing a relationship as it truly is; if jealousy is there, then there is something that is being overlooked or avoided.

In today's sexual society there is a notion that lovers should not mind the lover going off and making love with others; and this is promoted as a spiritual or unconditioned love. It is absolute nonsense and is a notion created by sexual man (and woman) to satisfy their lusting without being responsible for love.

◆

Dear Barry

I've always perceived God as the great ocean of love and considered that my problems would be solved by loving God as much as I was able. You have said that being is the solution to problems. This raises a question about a situation in my life at the moment.

My girlfriend has left me and is with another man. I see her occasionally as a friend and at other times try to catch glimpses of her around town. I seem addicted to the pain it causes me to see her with other men. I read a scripture once that says love knows no jealousy — but it's still a monster for me.

I try to send her love but this makes me think of her being with her new boyfriend who is probably able to love her and give to her in a way that I never could. Is it better to simply be rather than take the action of sending her my love?

William

William

For God's sake, man, face life as it is. The woman doesn't want you any more. She is finished with you. She loves someone else. It's over. She's not coming back. How can you want a woman who does not want you? What is the reality in your wanting? I ask you, could you possibly be happy anyway with anybody who did not want to be with you but wanted to be with someone else? Face the fact,

142 TO MAN IN TRUTH

man. Stop trying to send your love to her. It's meaningless, a self-deluding, self-indulgent distraction from the truth of the situation. And I suggest you don't see her any more as a friend. You are not up to having her as a friend. You are attached to her. And when you are attached to anyone or anything it is going to hurt you. You are tormenting yourself. Break completely with her. Do not go where she is or has been. Stop this madness.

The great ocean of love which is God can only be entered, realised, when you face life here as it is. To be able to face God as it is, you have to face life, the fact, as it is.

I know that you are a man of sensitivity, truly searching for the reality of your own being, the God within. But you must be more true to what I teach if you continue to write to me for help. To quote scriptures is nonsense unless you live them or they have real meaning. 'Love knows no jealousy' is a meaningless statement to anyone who is jealous, such as yourself. First you must deal with the jealousy before you can realise or live such love. And I tell you the way to deal with the jealousy, is to face the fact as I have told you.

Now get on with it.

◆

Dear Barry

My woman Amy and I have what we both recognise as a profound connection. We have known each other for several years now and gone through much together but our love has always shown us the way through. For a long time, although we loved each other she wasn't free to be with me. Finally we came together in a more permanent way and at last I felt we were really going to be together. Then she went away on holiday without me — due to work commitments I wasn't able to go too. While away she met another man with whom she has a deep attraction and came to love him as well. Although she says she still loves me, and I see that she does, she has invited the other man to come and stay with her for a few weeks to find out how 'real' their love is. She is prepared to throw away everything we have built together.

As I said, my love for Amy has withstood many difficulties in the past but this situation is causing me great suffering. I love Amy dearly but see that I can't bind love. She is a true and earnest woman and is not doing any of this to hurt me intentionally. What she is doing is right and I support her as much as I can but I can't handle the fact of the other man coming and living with her. Should I just 'wait in the wings' to see if she gets this man out of her system, meanwhile staying true to her as my love within? I really don't know what to do. Knowing the depth of our love for each other, I feel we will be united again, but why do I have to go through this pain?

Francis

Francis

You have to go through this pain, like everyone who says they love, because love between man and woman on this planet is invariably selfish. There are no exceptions — and there are no certainties. Everything must unfold by enactment, by doing, by being and the outcome is only what it is. But if you are true to love and truth, and not true to your self, your feelings or to Amy, you will find that all will work itself out.

It is possible that somewhere there is another woman making her way to you. It's also possible that you and Amy will get back together again. But life is all possibilities. If you are the man the words in your letter seem to describe, you will go through what has to be and emerge a more loving and noble man.

◆

Sex is God blind in existence.
Man's job is to make that God
conscious — which will turn
what was devilish
into love.

Dear Barry

How do I get rid of my sexual wanting? I see the beauty of woman just as she is but then I find myself wanting her. This causes me to suffer and also pushes woman away. I pray for help to get through this wanting.

Colin

Colin

The truth and fact is that man is attracted to woman more than anything else in his life. This is a natural magnetic attraction, natural meaning that it is created by God or the reality behind man and woman's existence.

Tragically man has been taught to lust after woman, which means to think about her body and private parts and thus stir his sexual wanting. This is perpetuated by the example of man's male friends and particularly by films, magazines and books writing salaciously about woman. To watch a sexual film, to read a sexual magazine story and to talk to your mates about woman, involves an action of imagination, or thinking, since no real woman is present — only man's thoughts and the inevitable lusting this creates. You will see from this that our whole modern society, based as it is on entertainment, actually promotes man's sexual wanting and fantastic desiring of woman.

The cure for sexual wanting is to actually love a real living woman; to refuse to read books or watch films that have sexual themes or scenes, and to never discuss woman sexually with other men. Something radical, you will see, has to be done, and that is it.

To love a real woman is not just to hop into bed with her and have sex with her. That again only perpetuates man's sexual wanting. To love a woman means to psychically, spiritually or intelligently reach down into the very depths of your being and realise and declare that she is what you truly love and desire more than anything else in the world. Unless this level of honesty is reached by you, you will continue having distractions which means giving in to thoughts about her and imagining what it is to love her, instead of simply and innocently loving her.

To love a woman is first of all to truly enjoy being in her presence; to truly enjoy holding her hand so that you are conscious every moment of the simple pleasure of being able to have physical contact with this extraordinary subject of your fundamental God-given desire. When you take her in your arms, to delight in the psychic smell of her; when you kiss her hair, her cheek or her shoulder, and when you make love with her, you consciously *be* this simple pleasure — and all this without one single selfish sexual thought about 'wanting' her. This is the other side of the curative equation.

If you are not with woman then you must never think about her. While you are dispelling your lust you must avoid, as much as possible, looking at her beautiful form in the street because your lust will look first before your eyes even register what they are seeing. The lust will turn your perception into the perpetuation of man's and society's greatest cause of unhappiness — sexual greed and sexual dishonesty.

Don't tell me you don't have a real woman to love. The only reason she is not with you is because you continue to lust after her and sexually scare her (a real woman) away. If you approach women with the innocence that I have described which is not looking for a conclusion (as sex or excitement), you will find they tend to respond; not in a sexual way but as a simple exchange. And this particularly if you avoid speaking to her from your personality and simply address her from the reality of your fundamental love of her, which is in every single male, obscured in most cases by his lusting mind and excitable emotions.

◆

Dear Barry

I am a zoologist spending a year conducting research in an isolated area in Africa. As I am living alone, I am using this time to develop a regular habit of meditation for the first time in my life — and I am using your 'Meditation' and 'Stillness Is The Way' books to guide me.

There is another habit, though, which is a source of growing unease and which I would like to ask you about. I find that every week or so I get quite strong sexual urges and I then indulge in sexual fantasies and masturbation. I don't feel particularly good about this, yet I don't seem able to stop either. In 'Stillness Is The Way' you say, 'If your problem is drink or sex or whatever, you should really indulge your desire. Get into it. Don't be moderate. Get stuck into it! That way you will fill your desire and then you'll only have the habit to deal with. And habit is brittle: it can be broken once you've reached the peak of the desire. But this will only work if you know what you are doing and stay conscious of what you are doing.'

What I'd like to ask is, does this apply to the solitary sexual urge as well, or is there perhaps something you might care to say about this particular habit?

Frank

Frank

The strong sexual urges come from past fantasising when you did have woman to make love with. Now, when you don't have her, the fantasising habit goes on. And the result is fantastic or phantom lovemaking — masturbation. Masturbation ceases as the fantasising stops. Do *not* fantasise about her or her private part. Don't read sexual books. While you do you will suffer as you have described.

There is the divine female inside you. She wants you to be a real man, not to give in to fantasies of her. Use the time you are without a partner, with meditation, to break the compulsive habit that keeps all men from *realising* her. Do this and in time the divine principle within will manifest through some woman to love you. But you must give up your affair with fantasy woman. Otherwise you will draw an emotional, unhappy woman.

Masturbation and thinking about woman sexually is a compulsion, not a desire. There is nothing material or physical in it, only self-love which is impossible. You break the compulsive habit by not thinking and descending deeper and deeper into the black, the nothing, you call Me inside your body. Be still. That's what your isolation is for. Stiller and stiller, into the silence within.

Several months later Frank wrote again to Barry.

Dear Barry Long

Thank you very much for your reply to my question about sexual fantasising — I found it most illuminating. In the last few months, however, a different problem — or a different aspect of the same problem — has arisen.

After I wrote to you, the images of women as a sexual stimulant started to fade away, but were replaced by more disturbing images of a sado-masochistic kind. For many years I have felt a certain sexual 'edge' to paintings of martyrdom and descriptions of torture, but now they have come to occupy the centre of my sexual imaginings. Obviously the thing is not to indulge such fantasies, but they keep recurring.

Is there anything to be gained from looking deeper into why this is happening, or is it best to simply let such fantasies slide out of consciousness as soon as they slide in, without any reflection as to where they're coming from? I had thought that my Irish Catholic upbringing with its glorification of suffering and martyrdom — along with the fact that my very earliest memory is being smacked on my penis by my irate mother when she discovered me playing with it in the bath — might have something to do with this disturbing association of pain and pleasure. Whatever it is, I'm starting to feel myself increasingly in the grip of a dark and possibly dangerous force.

I feel rather at a loss about the whole business, so I'd appreciate it very much if you have anything to say on the matter.

Frank

PS Apart from the above difficulties, I do have a strong sense that my isolation does indeed have a purpose — to enable me to go, as you say, stiller and stiller into the silence within.

Frank

Your Irish Catholic upbringing, with its appalling glorification of suffering and martyrdom, will have contributed much to your difficulty. So will the smacking of your penis; the penis being the organ of love and the mother being a man's first love. Religion is supposed to be about love, not suffering. It invokes the inner unrealised knowledge of psychic union which all human beings are seeking — and due to the ignorance of priests and interpreters, it introduces an emotional or selfish drive into outer satisfaction or achievement.

Regarding the sado-masochistic level you've encountered. Yes, this is in your subconscious where all emotional hurts and former indoctrinations lie. As one aspect of the ignorant sexual drive — the emotional/mental — is addressed, the next more subtle level appears. This continues in the spiritual life until sex transforms into love. As love is psychic, beneath the subconscious, union as clarity or peace from restlessness is reached.

The dark and possibly dangerous force you feel is only your self, your past, arising because you are descending towards the psyche, the harmony that is called Life or God.

Be still. Do not fight it. Stillness is the way. Fight it and you give it strength. You are stronger in stillness than any past that can arise in you — even though it may appear threatening and terrifying. Be still. Know that I am with you in silence, the stillness within. Every man (and woman) must face the emotional past of their own self, what they have been. That self is what is called in occult terms, the 'Guardian of the Threshold'. If I cannot face my self, the ignorance I have been, how can I face and join my God? That is the divine justice. Yes, your isolation is the means — and stillness is the way.

◆

Barry

Oh what a vicious, damning entity is sex. Wanting, doubting and judging its way to rise as a wave on a still ocean. I have often acknowledged the power of this sex but all too regularly ignored its presence. Life has given me a wonderful partner and seemingly endless opportunities to face the sex in me.

My partner has reflected this to me again tonight. I must acknowledge that while eighty per cent of the time I can see the good, all too often I find my mind challenged by sexual images, insecurities, expressions.

I was recently 'swamped' by a wave when I read a text on pornography. I knew what would be said. I felt my trembling body and active mind — but I read it. This was a climactic action as for the next few days I endeavoured to see the good and believed I was doing so. However my woman had the courage to point out the truth that psychically I had moved and taken a position of resistance, despite my verbal denials. Exposing the sex to the truth was a turning point and I have now taken the action of writing to you.

Michael

Michael

It seems to me you know what you have to do and are doing your best to live that. It's not clear whether the text you read was actually pornographic but you must know that pornography is just too powerful a magnet for any man endeavouring to live a life of love to flirt with. Better to look away or close the book. Sex is only God blind in existence and my job as man is to make that God conscious which will turn what was devilish into love. I'm not talking ideals. I'm talking fact and you and I must do it.

◆

Dear Barry

As in many men my sexual energy has been repressed and dominated by fantasies for most of my life. Often I have expressed it through masturbation instead of actually making love to a woman. After hearing your 'Making Love' tapes I saw much I had not seen before and felt more ready to love. After this, on the fairly rare occasions I was with a woman, I tried to make love more consciously. I still continued to masturbate though, as I was more often alone.

I am now experiencing a recurring difficulty. Over the last few months several beautiful and loving women have moved in and out of my life and I have felt each of them to be a gift from God. But when we came to make love the same thing happened: my genitals felt cut off and dead and I was unable to get an erection, even though it was lovely to be with the woman. Currently I have a new woman who is very loving and with whom I would like to have a relationship. But the same thing is happening. I want to love her completely as a man should, with strength and tenderness. Can you help?

Parahito

Parahito

The not getting of an erection, as I mention in my 'Making Love' tapes, is often due to the transition from the old sexual/fantasising habits to starting to make love. The cutting off in the genital area, the deadness you speak of, is caused by the old habits which literally separated the man from his natural ability/enjoyment of sensuous expression. Masturbation contributes to all this through its fantastic notions of making love to a woman who is not there — a denial of the reality of love which can only be made with a physical woman.

All that you have been through and the overall tone of your letter shows that you have learned the lesson of the pain of sex and are now in the process of leaving that behind. The fact that woman has come to you, as you say, 'a gift from God' symbolises the assent of the divine woman, the power — and your loving words, your worthiness. To say that you wish to love your current woman, 'completely as a man should, with strength and tenderness', is sufficient. That is the way, love is the way. Do that with one woman despite the sometimes heavy going, and you have the help which you ask for.

I must say to you that the whole sannyasin* notion of love, of moving from one woman to another, is a denial of love and leads to the sexual manipulation of woman and causes the very problems you have mentioned. To reverse the situation you must stay with one woman and work at it together with love and honesty as I teach.

◆

* Sannyasin: traditionally a Hindu renunciate but in this context a disciple of Bhagwan Shree Rajneesh, later Osho, an Eastern master who advocated sexual freedom as part of his teaching.

Dear Barry

Can you give me some help with something that has been troubling me for some time?

I can't stop going to prostitutes. I am addicted to experiencing the variety and the enjoyment of the woman being there to please me and me not having to do anything. I am okay for a little while but then the urge builds up in me again and won't let me rest until I give in to it. I know it's sex and not love. I want to stop but I don't seem to be able to.

Malcolm

Malcolm

You are sexually indulgent of your self. You will see this in your own description of being addicted to going to prostitutes, the need for variety and her pleasing you, rather than you having to take responsibility for love and pleasing the woman. The irresistible compulsion (to go again), as it builds up in a short while after being with a prostitute, is precisely the same as the irresistible compulsion to masturbate. You are masturbating in these women, and in woman.

You must start taking responsibility if you are serious in your desire to be more conscious. You are allowing your mind and emotions to think about and ruminate on woman during your daily life and on the expectation of sexual gratification in the future in the way that you describe — by going to prostitutes or masturbating. Your sexuality is living in the future. To cure the addiction you must give this up. Be one-pointed about what you don't want which is to be manipulated by your sexual addiction and that means not engaging in sexual thought and rumination.

◆

*Making love with woman is a
pleasure and a privilege.*

Dear Barry

At this moment in my life, there is a deep question within me regarding my partnership.

I have been married for twenty years and during this time have raised three children, worked hard and experienced a lot of what life has to offer. However there seems to be a deep longing to be truly loved.

I love my partner very much and yet she seems to be always on guard or not totally relaxed. It is as though she thinks that if she gave herself to love, I would leave her. All I can say to this is that after twenty years of marriage, there's a fair chance that I'll be around for another twenty.

I would love her to just let go and relax. I have spoken to her about this but perhaps after all these years together it becomes more difficult to have objective communication.

We rarely make love and when I ask her about this she says that I am too sexual.

Now this is so on some occasions when I am in my 'over the top' high energy, but I believe that deep down she is afraid to make love with me. Saying that I am too sexual has allowed her an escape road. I do not push on these matters, just walk with her, give her hugs and talk. You spoke on a tape about not suiting each other and I am wondering if this is the case with us.

The crazy part about this is that when I am away from her, she is so loving and soft to me during our telephone conversations.

I am perplexed. Women surely are one of the greatest mysteries of life. How do you see this situation? Do I consider myself and move on, or do I stay and just be with her?

Brendan

Brendan

You are obviously looking at your situation with your partner very closely. It's not altogether a fair chance that you'll be around for another twenty years when you ask, 'Do I consider myself and move on?' It's troubling you. And rightly so.

It's not clear whether your partner is in my teaching but there seems that implication, or perhaps she has heard some of my work? When a woman refuses to make love because 'you are too sexual', in my teaching this means that if she continues to enjoy living with you, her task of love then is to show you how not to be 'too sexual'. And this by being in a situation of lovemaking. Here she can have you desist and point out in the moment where your sexuality is excessive, so that you are able to address it and take the necessary action within yourself to subdue it without repression. This is the task of true love between man and woman, whether the problem be his or hers.

It becomes difficult, as you say, after many years together but really that's no excuse once both parties hear the truth of love and are willing to live it.

Have you and your woman listened together to my 'Making Love' tapes and agreed to apply them?

It seems to me, and this is not a criticism, that she is loving and soft during your telephone conversations because you're too far away for this to encourage you physically. She can afford to be loving then. But the question remains, how about when you're there? Each has to take his and her responsibility for love, not just toss it on to the other.

Even so, it is your story I'm hearing and not your wife's. There has to be two sides and you have to listen very seriously to what she says and be prepared to take remedial action for the sake of your partnership.

◆

166 TO MAN IN TRUTH

Dear Barry

I am with a lovely woman, Vicky, and we have been practising making love as you teach it for more than a couple of years now. We find that what you say is true, we are discovering more love and beauty together. However at times I still find it difficult to distinguish between sensuality and sexuality.

I don't want to repress my natural passion and the pure sensuous enjoyment of making love. It is my delight to 'just love her' as I have heard you describe at your meetings. But as I go into my passion, and particularly as I feel Vicky's pleasure increasing, I get lost in the sensuality and excitement takes me over.

Is there anything you can say about this, Barry?

Ken

Ken

The difference between sensuality and sex is that sex is impatient and seeks some end for itself. Sensuality, although highly passionate, is not impatient and enjoys the sheer sensuality as love of woman every moment of the physical contact without needing an end or a climax. Force is impatience and excitement — sex.

The answer is in your statement, 'I get lost in the sensuality'. Then don't. Keep your presence. Ask Vicky to help you. She will know when you are beginning to get excited or lost. Ask her to tell you. She should not allow you inside her while you are excited. You can pull back from this and with practice will discover a steady sensual pleasure of love that does not need to race ahead of the moment.

◆

Hello Barry

Using a condom when making love reduces the pleasure for me and makes my penis less sensitive to what's going on. Is this true for everybody? If so, could you explain why? My lover says making love is a psychic experience and it doesn't matter if you wear a condom or not.

I would like to thank you for all you have taught me through your tapes, books and lectures and for the love and stillness that has helped me to get closer to life.

Giles

Giles

Is it the intelligence in your penis that wrote your letter or your selfish mind?

Making love with woman is a pleasure, a privileged pleasure, even if I am simply caressing or holding her intimately to me, let alone entering her body. If I am looking for a pleasure beyond the moment, that is if my penis has a condom on and I am anxious or ruminative about this, I will be in my mind. The pleasure of being in the woman's body will be reduced, not by the condom but by my being selfishly in my own mind. I must make love wholeheartedly, that is with my whole body, and leave my silly mind out of it.

I would not be using a condom unless I needed to. Perhaps you should examine why you are using a condom and then feeling unhappy about it. You will discover some dishonesty in yourself through this. Your woman in this respect is more in her body than you.

Thank you for the expressions in the rest of your letter and I know you are earnest in your endeavour to love rightly.

◆

Dear Barry

My present partner Gail and I came together quite recently. I have never experienced such beautiful love for a woman before. She says it is the same for her. Our lovemaking is quite exquisite and she has really opened to me for which I am deeply grateful.

Prior to being with me, Gail had an unhappy relation-ship with a man who was sexually abusive. I am very conscious of loving her rightly and not introducing sex into her as I want to heal her painful past and not in any way add to it. Orgasm is not a problem for me, Barry, and we often make love without me having to come. Before I do orgasm though, I increase my tempo beyond my usual movements in lovemaking. I'm wondering if this is all right or whether it is putting something into my woman.

I would be grateful for any light you could throw on this subject and thank you for your 'Making Love' tapes.

Stuart

Stuart

The increase in tempo is all right. As you are able to finish at times without orgasm, you will know what you are doing. So tell her that you are now going to orgasm, give her your essence, your love. From what you say, this will please her, for you love one another and you are sensitive to not introducing sex (as selfish force or unconscious sexual indulgence) into her. Woman's fulfilment is to receive the man who truly loves her. She should open herself psychically (which will translate slowly into physically) at these times to take all — and that will help her to release the past hurts and uncertainties and help the Man in you, he who is behind the overt passion, to take them from her.

◆

Dear Barry

Yvonne and I got together a few months ago. I am now staying with her and looking at the prospect of moving in. Yvonne is the most loving and open woman I have been with but we both seem to be experiencing mood swings and fluctuating emotions in our love-life. Our lovemaking is often very beautiful but after it's over I can feel sad which makes me withdraw from her. This disturbs her and makes her feel she wants to get away from me. Then I feel even worse.

Another thing I find very disturbing is the fact that Yvonne has been a sannyasin in the past and has had a lot of sexual experience. This makes me feel insecure and any demand on her part to make love also makes me withdraw — there can be an appetite in her that I find distasteful. Again my withdrawal arouses feelings of rejection in her. But often we are intensely and passionately in love and deeply attracted to each other. At these times our lovemaking is ecstatic and there is more love between us than I have ever known with a woman.

Still, I find I am assailed with doubts. I don't seem to be able to shake off the shadow of reservation. Yvonne can be very strong in her love and when the shadow is upon me she says we should make love to get me out of it, but I feel this to be wrong. I'm confused Barry. I'm confused by the intensity of feelings this love seems to provoke in me. I love her and yet I fear we won't be able to make it together. Mostly I fear that I simply can't love enough, although I would like to be man enough to take her on.

Ross

Ross

We are provided with people to love and to help us through but it is the love behind all that we are actually serving. This love is an intelligence, the intelligence beyond person, in this matter.

What you describe in your letter are ups and downs, the fluctuations of feelings, or self. This is inevitable, so don't be discouraged. You just have to keep persevering and loving as best as you can. It is not only you who has things to heal, deep past hurts, fears and anxieties to be opened up to the light of love and intelligent scrutiny. Yvonne also has much of this in her. And of course in both cases, it is basically sexual. That is coming from past addiction to pleasure as the excitement of making love in the old selfish way.

Post-coital tristesse, sadness after making love (coming), is an almost universal experience. It arises from the old way of making love, self-love. So there's no great mystery in the fluctuations you are both experiencing. You go down, she gets hurt and wants to get away. You go up, she gets excited, you're both excited, you make excitable love and down you go again, the condition of each other's psyche affecting the other. Tristesse, sorrow, disappears from coitus as excitement (or addiction to the old pleasure) is dissolved. And it is only dissolved by perseverance in love, by not serving your feelings. It took effort to become depressed or unhappy, and it takes effort (for a time) to get rid of it.

Yes, if you make love for yourself to get out of the shadow, it is trying to get and it is sex — and you know this. Yvonne must give up the demand to make love. It is from her past and particularly her past conditioning associated with the sannyasin notion of love. At the same time she must be available for love but not give in to your sexuality, or her own, when it is there. Quieten each other down. It doesn't take long. Then begin again.

You should tell Yvonne when you are disturbed and what's going on. But you must get it out quickly and not dwell on it. You're supposed to just get it out but the danger is that you'll start indulging, emotionalising and enjoying the regurgitated feeling. Do not go into the troublesome stuff inside you on your own. Stay in your senses. Stop self-considering, thinking. It's a lovely day in your senses, but never in your self unless you're indulging your self. Such indulgence means that tomorrow you'll have another downer. There's no opposite to joy or being in the senses.

Yvonne must remember that the big emphasis in the sannyasin way of life was to be true to your self, to go with your feelings which are your emotions. This is not the truth but she will have this conditioning in her. Both of you at all times must be true to the situation. The situation is that you are in partnership to enjoy being together because you love one another. Every personal defence, position and opinion comes from a feeling. You must put love first.

The resistance in you is only the monitor who is always looking back or looking forward. The reality is your body and it does what it does every moment.

◆

Dear Barry

I have difficulty controlling ejaculation when making love.

I'm aware that the very attempt to control the ejaculation is a distraction that takes me away from being with my woman in the moment. But the whole thing can become a vicious circle.

Often, the beauty of what I am experiencing precipitates the ejaculation. Sometimes it is my sensing of my partner's rising pleasure and my desire to delight her further. It seems to require great presence to 'keep it together' in the face of the beauty I perceive in woman.

What can I do, Barry? Is it a matter of greater presence — or greater sexual mastery? I have such a longing to truly reach and fulfil my partner.

Ben

Ben

'Premature' ejaculation, in the situation you describe, is something that all men must face when they are with a woman who opens up completely to them. The nature of things is that as a woman's pleasure increases, so does the man's. Finally when her pleasure is at its 'high point' this is supposed to pull the very essence, his semen, out of the man into her open and waiting womb. But the search for God in physical lovemaking is not about this. The search for God requires man to put God (whatever that is) before his own self-ish sensory pleasure. His purpose in making love is to practise increasing his threshold of containment under the beautiful pressure of his woman's rising pleasure. I am not suggesting ideals: every man will ejaculate from time to time under this enormous vacuous pull of woman's pleasure.

It seems to me that there is still a movement of your mind when you are making love to your woman. By movement I mean the sheer knowledge or knowing that you are in her and that she is reaching a high point of pleasure. The slightest movement of the mind, of knowing, in this situation will cause ejaculation. It would be a good idea when your woman's passion hits a certain point that you know to be 'dangerous' for you, to pause, remaining in her, but *not* allowing any mind movement. The more you practise this pause, the more you will find the duration of it reduces. Finally it can be simply, or seemingly, a split-second pause and then you are okay to keep going. Of course it is important to have your woman's co-operation and for her not to feel you are leaving her when you pause.

As you practise this you will find that you are gradually detaching yourself from the action. Your imagination or memory of where you are or what you are doing must be more and more left behind. This will leave the body only making the love and gradually reduce the feeling that makes you ejaculate. When the body alone makes love and there is no person or self as imagination or memory involved, it is called absence and then divine love and union as a continuous exquisite delight for both is possible.

There are, of course, degrees of premature ejaculation which all men suffer from at some time in their lives.

The most troublesome, especially for youths and young men, is that ejaculation which happens as soon as their penis touches woman's private part or even before. This is due to young men's constant thinking about sex and woman which keeps them in a heightened condition of expectation, needing only the slightest affirmation from the woman's presence to actuate. Then there is ejaculation that occurs very quickly after entry into the woman, and so on. In that sense I wouldn't call your ejaculation premature, since it seems to happen after your loving of your woman has brought her to a rising point of passion. So it would be good for you not to regard yourself as ejaculating prematurely, for these thoughts influence the responses.

A finer point is to examine what you are doing in the rest of your life. Are you talking and chatting needlessly; do you make unnecessary phone calls; are you watching too much television or too many videos and are you too identified with your work, so that you tend to lose yourself in it? Excess in these areas builds up a momentum of excitement in your self or mind and the momentum will contribute to the lack of containment in lovemaking. Your whole life is about cultivating spiritual power and neither lovemaking nor any other activity in your life can be isolated from this purpose. The life must be lived as a whole, not in enthusiastic or boring fragments.

◆

Barry

In the last session of the meeting at Santa Fe, an important question arose in me regarding my relationship and growth as a man. Time ran out and my question wasn't answered. My sadness and self-pity turned to anger and I cursed your name and your teaching all the way home. I have now let these emotions go for the most part.

The noble man whom you speak of and which I am — whose wonderful job on earth is to love woman, to let her feel his love, to love the past and the sex out of her with his loving penis and create the environment in which she can flower as woman — this is the man with whom I often feel connected.

Making love is an exchange of psychic energies. What should I do when I am not feeling so loving but am filled with wanting, horny sex? Should I then fill my woman with more sex and past when I should be drawing it out of her? Is it better psychically and energetically that I masturbate instead — or go to another woman who wants sex, or a prostitute — rather than infect my partner with my sex? And what is my woman's role then? Is she to refuse me and my sex, or receive me in an act of love?

Larry

Larry

Where was the noble man when you were cursing my name and my teaching? How can you ask the subsequent questions in your letter about loving woman when there is such unloving emotional fury in your self? Did you love enough, did it even occur to you when you wrote, 'I have now let those emotions go for the most part', to withdraw the curse you put upon me?

Why do you not write to me of your love of life, your gratitude to God for what has come to you through my teaching and being with me? How could you love woman when you are so centred on yourself?

To answer the questions in the final paragraph of your letter: it's no good waiting until your horny self takes over. You have to address the cause of it long before. And that means now. When you ask me should you go and masturbate, go to a prostitute or give your sex to your partner, that is your horny self thinking and speaking and getting subtle excitement from such propositions. Propositions are what you have stated, not questions. How often do you think about masturbating, going to a prostitute or having sex with your woman? Stop that sort of thinking and your horny self will deflate and die.

Your woman will never be able to receive your sexual obsession in an act of love. That is another sexual and selfish fantasy.

Now get on with it. Get your mind off your penis, your self — and live *giving*, not trying to get.

◆

Barry

Your teaching has brought so much good into our lives and today I really want to thank you.

You are the only one who speaks about lovemaking. Sometimes when we make love there is no climax and no ecstasy but afterwards we feel astonishingly easy and harmonious and our life together is then good. Sometimes it also happens that both of us or one of us does not feel any sweetness in the act of lovemaking; it can even be painful or at least not sweet, although we are both present. This has happened quite often and as a reaction we engaged in excitement and sex. This then led to depression on my side. In our experience it is not the woman who gets depressed from sex.

If we just keep our minds out and let the bodies make love it can easily bring about a sensation of sweetness which is quite regularly followed by a hardening of the penis and excitation on both sides. When the penis becomes tight it may be felt as a tension or as a pain in the vagina. We then stop and pause and for a while lovemaking can go on like a 'stop-and-go thing'. If we don't feel any sweetness we usually stop and it seems as if nothing good has happened.

In our experience lovemaking does have ups and downs, it is not constant. How can we know if all this is due to our sexual past or to 'not fitting'*? If it is our sexual past we need patience. If we don't fit each other

---

* Fitting and suiting: fitting — to be sexually compatible; suiting — to be emotionally and mentally compatible.

— what to do? We love each other and this love has become clearer and stronger and more beautiful due to your help.

Richard

Richard

Regarding the matters raised in your letter, you should both be as easy as you can when you come together to make love, leaving everything in the past behind. You should both acknowledge, as much as you can, that where love is concerned you have nothing more in your lives to be anxious about.

Richard must not bring any aspects of stress in his work into your interaction. And Rachel must know that there is nothing left of the past in her, so that she is innocent — which is the truth. You, Rachel, are literally God in female form, the stream up which man and your own consciousness climb to God or paradise. Delight in this knowledge. Live it, be it as much as possible while you are making love. The man will respond to you, for you are the existential course of love. You appear in a woman's form but just inside that form you are this beauteous state.

Both of you must make love with the whole of your body and not just with parts of it. The whole puts every-thing back into context. It is only when we take things out of context that we upset the harmony that we are.

Give up concern about your 'sexual past' and any

notion of 'not fitting'. You love one another. You enjoy being together and loving together. No more questioning or anxieties about what I have said at the meetings (about making love). Your love for each other is enough.

◆

Barry

First, my deepest gratitude for your teaching. You have made a tremendous change in my life and consciousness. And I believe my children and those I love have benefited. I have lived your suggestions through times of doubt and turmoil and life has always provided, as you have said. I have got my life straight and each morning I give thanks for another day of loving.

I would like some clarification on the tantric practices you have advised. My lover and I have listened to your 'Making Love' tapes. For the last year and a half we have been making love this way to the best of our ability. We both realised the difference between sex and love, but in our lovemaking orgasm would frequently occur. In the last few months we have both arrived at a point where we do not experience orgasm in the usual sense. I, in particular, feel multiple subtle peaks like orgasm but with no ejaculation. More and more I feel I'm living the reality you expressed in the tapes. There is no technique on my part, other than simply relaxing into the lovemaking. We are both completely in the present with no mental images, or striving, to separate us.

But there seems to be a problem. In the last few weeks my lover has been feeling a continuous uncomfortable congestion in her uterus and vagina. There is no indication of a medical problem. A spiritual woman who was my lover for a brief period in the past showed me a technique in which a woman could ejaculate. I showed this to my current partner and she was able to do it with the result of removing the feeling of congestion.

After careful consideration we both feel that this ejaculation is not part of true lovemaking. It has the same effect of seeking orgasm — pushing us apart and we lose the sense of deep connection. Pondering the dilemma, we have postulated that the problem may be an effect of what you have described as the psychic 'maleness' injected into my woman by past improper lovemaking by me and others and that it is a layer of psyche we must pass through as we enter love more deeply. Is this the explanation? What are we doing wrong and how should we proceed in the spirit of your teaching?

Mike

Mike

Female ejaculation sounds like a bit of a circus, an interesting male performance. You don't need it.

Otherwise if you are living and loving in the way that attracted you both to my teaching, you are doing nothing wrong. It's just life. You will pass through any difficulties. Nothing lasts — only the good and the right.

◆

Dear Barry

Both my partner Alice and I have gained enormously from your teaching. Our relationship has become richer and more joyful and for that I offer you my deepest thanks. I am writing now to ask your advice about lovemaking.

For some time Alice and I have been putting into practice what you teach in your lovemaking tapes. Through this we have reached at times a greater love and fineness than we had known before. But Alice, although she is always willing to make love with me, often experiences a dullness and lack of response within. This has driven us both to go for orgasm to create some sort of result although we know this really isn't the way. We both sense that there is a profundity to lovemaking we have not been able to experience together yet. I feel in some way I have failed to delight my woman and bring her deeper into her own love.

I still wish to persevere with your teaching because I feel it to be right but I really don't know how to get through this. What can I do next?

Craig

Craig

You must love her more. You must woo her every day. When you are with her you must speak of the beauty that you find in her. You must tell her how much you appreciate living with her and the delight that she gives you in loving you.

It seems to me, that this is what you are not doing except when it occurs to you. Wooing a woman is a full-time activity, just like you wooed her when you first met her or first began to make love. It is the avoidance or ignorance of wooing that creates the familiarity, the casualness that comes between man and woman.

She has to be treated by you as a woman — and a woman is made for love and for being told of her man's love for her. To this she cannot help but respond — although she herself must also practise this acknowledgement of love when she sees it in her man.

◆

*For man the love of woman is the
love of God in existence.*

Barry Long

Master of Love
Thank you. Thank you for your love, your wisdom, your teaching. Thank you for teaching me how to love woman rightly. It is wondrous. It is sublime. It is all that in my ignorance I dreamed and hoped that love should be — and more. It's beyond imagining.

Thank you for teaching me how to live the divine life. Of course, I have much to be free of, but it is, by the grace of God, only a question of time. Should I die today, no matter.

I have no questions about life, truth, God, death and love. I am surrendered.

I am aware of the responsibility of my life and am deeply grateful. It is an extraordinary privilege to live this wonderful life free of problems, free of doubt.

Thank you for your love, dear Master.

With love in my heart now, with eternal gratitude, with joy that is simple, innocent, I thank thee, Barry Long.

Robin

◆

Hello Barry

Firstly I would like to say thank you for everything I have received over the years I have been with your teaching.

As I live the truth more and more I have seen my life go from a mess, to good, to great to beautiful. Now life has 'produced' for me a most beautiful woman, Laura, who loves God, is straight and true and knows her purpose for living. I feel I have met the woman I was born to meet. It is as if meeting her is the end of a dream and the start of my life. It is so wonderful to love so intensely and want nothing, only to totally respect her and protect her if needed. I love her totally as Woman and sometimes find her beautifully nothing, as her being is so much love and not personality.

Every day I find myself asking life to bring me what I need to make me more real so I may serve love. I am still physically in the same world but nothing is the same. Nothing means much to me any more, only living my life for Thee, the beauty within Me, God. It is not always easy but when I am getting it right my life is more beautiful.

Yes Barry, I have finally found something in life I will die for. Woman as God has entered my life and it is my privilege to give it all up for her. I have seen that if I cannot do it for true woman, I cannot do it for anything. And I can and am doing it. I live now only to become more real, more the noble man you talk of. I know him and know he is my right 'destiny'.

I am truly blessed and full of gratitude.

Adrian

A few months later he wrote again.

Hello Barry

It is a divine privilege to communicate at such a true and real level with woman. I am seeing it is what I have truly desired all my life but I have not known it before. The beauteous divine consciousness of pure woman — how I love She. The love she is is so utterly undeniable, so completely desirable, I am drawn to it like a moth to its own destruction in the flame.

I am denying my old self expression, avoiding 'not right' company so as to starve my self — there's not much truth or God consciously lived among my work colleagues. The pressure from them to join in, go out, or joke too much is right and keeps me straight. It's good to see it rarely affects me or removes me from the knowledge of my love and purpose. It is so true — man really must give it all up for his beloved in order to truly serve love and God. It's not always easy and sometimes it burns me, but always behind me is the all-encircling presence that never leaves, that is my truth, my being. When self rises, my being is always there behind, watching and keeping me in peace beneath the storm, just as the ocean is undisturbed below the surface waves. There is less and less desire to inflict my self on another. In my giving up, I am blessed with a new and inner steadiness.

It's beautiful, Barry. I perceive that I am up here looking out of my eyes at the world, and inside Woman has a rope attached to me and is ever pulling me down, down. How blessed I am that my woman is so committed to God, truth and love and will not allow my self to interfere. My whole life has changed. I live my life now to serve this divine love as best I can and not for my self. So beautiful has true woman shown herself to be, that my whole impulse is to be with this God-woman so we may serve life in our being together. And yet in this wondrous golden love, Laura and I know that it is all utterly impersonal. Love truly is the great transformer, the only thing worthy of true sacrifice, the only thing I can give my self up for.

Another effect of this love is that I see the woman in my past relationship rise up into my consciousness. I feel a sadness at the hurt I inflicted upon her in my ignorance, as I now have contacted the beautiful woman she is within me and recognise the love she gave so constantly and selflessly. I am endeavouring to let this go.

Even if Laura and I were to part, as one day we may, I can never go back, never give up. I have been shown the power and beauty of woman.

Adrian

◆

Hello Barry

I just had to inform you that after ten years of being with your teaching, I've had enough. Enough of this selfish persistent sexual self. I am blessed and feel grateful to be with a woman who is helping me keep straight and yes, Barry, I truly adore her.

Since my switch from sex to love she has opened to me like a flower to the sun and at forty-five years old I have finally realised what it is to love woman.

I wish to express my gratitude to you or the Most High, Barry, and trust that this love continues to go deeper.

Steve

◆

Dear Barry

I am writing to express the eternal gratitude that is in me, for the love that you are and how your being this love, expressing and demonstrating this love, has penetrated to my very being and transformed my life and loving.

I have so much gratitude in me for all that is. Gratitude that such a love has entered me, and for the privilege to be loving and being loved by Claire. This love is tearing me apart, relentless and so beautiful and the self is powerless under the onslaught of the merciless demand of this love.

I am amazed at the ever-urgent demand of this love to be one-pointed. I had a realisation the other day that I love only Woman. But then I watched as divine love came into me and turned all of my realisation into the one point, focusing my love of all women into the love of Claire. I am only here on this earth to love her completely and devotedly for as long as this love is here in me.

I am blessed by this self-consuming love within me. I delight in this love. I delight in just loving Claire and being this love for her. I love giving in everything I do to become simpler and more humble each day.

Daniel

◆

Dear Barry

As you know my life has changed radically in the last few weeks and much that I held dear was taken from me. As I left everything willingly for the truth inside me, the Bhagavati* revealed herself to me. I didn't have a vision as such but the knowledge of profound love began to arise in me for a woman called Elizabeth, whom I had recently met but not in a romantic circumstance. As this love began to dawn on me my mind began to freak out completely. I knew my mind was speeding up in its terror so I went into Me.

After about an hour I had a profound and powerful communication from deep inside. It arose in me like a huge black presence that had always been there and had just surfaced for the communication. It said or communicated rather, 'Yes! This the Bhagavati. Yes! Your place is to be with this woman, Elizabeth. I am She. Love me through her body!'

It was so strong there was no room for doubt nor has there been since. I have done everything practically to enable me to be with this woman totally. I now live with her.

Since my realisation I have had a knowledge of a profundity of love I didn't know existed, let alone thought possible. My sense is that dealing with pain and suffering as a consequence of love is past. What is truly new and devastating to my self is the confrontation of affirmation: seeing the undeniable power of love working. Standing in the face of the exquisite knowledge of love destroys my self in a way I haven't experienced before.

---

* Bhagavati: God in female form — the divine female principle endeavouring to manifest consciously in every woman.

Being with Elizabeth is living the paradox of impersonal love. I love her with intense devotion, great resonance and a huge knowledge of gratitude. While my knowledge is of the impersonality of the love, there is also great intimacy with that. It is such a total experience, such a swift movement and change. And yet there is very little to say about it. Living it is more than enough.

Gilbert

◆

Dear Barry

Some time ago at one of your seminars I spoke to you about my desire to love woman and how I had been without a woman as a partner for many years.

In your reply you said, among other things, that she was definitely coming to me.

This letter is to let you know that she has! Helen has come to live with me. This is very beautiful for me. She is living love and being together is wonderful for us both.

I see that this is the opportunity to really live more fully the truth that I have seen in my life and that I have come to through absorbing your realised truth in particular, over many years. I am more in touch with the truth of being and being ordinary.

In one of your recent Gold Coast tapes you talked of discarding the books and tapes and simply living it. I can connect with this. Since being with Helen I have hardly been moved to listen to your tapes which for years I've done almost every day — because here is the living woman to love.

I am grateful that you have loved woman without sex (thought) because that is quite a task. This is what I desire to actualise in my life more and more. You have made it easier for everyone else, as do the men who have heard your truth and are living it.

Charles

◆

Dear Barry

I am writing to tell you how good my life is. I have been with Isabel for nearly two years now and our love together is beautiful. When we came together at first, I had realised woman as the living reflection of God, a power greater than any man can be. Isabel appeared as this woman, the woman of my dreams that every man longs for.

The test for me as a man has been to be with this love while its great power transforms my life. Prior to meeting Isabel, I had been living in what I could best describe as limbo, compromise with my self and seemingly with every area of my life. Choicelessly I gave up selfish fear for the love of the golden woman that I had seen in her. I then realised the immortality of love that is within me and everyone, the great life that is deathless.

I gradually realised that I had been reborn into a new life. I had only heard of this in Christian terms and had no idea what it really meant. What I did know was that my life was changing.

The power of the love I had realised was gradually starting to straighten out my life, and is still continuing to do so. To begin with this was a painful and often distressing process as the old was being destroyed in my psyche to make way for the new. What made it bearable was the undeniable rightness of what was happening and the knowledge that love was behind it all. From this I realised the truth of passion: when I throw my selfishness onto the pyre, by dying to it, it generates my passion for life and love.

After nearly two years I have a wonderful life living with the woman I love and adore. Her presence has helped me to build a new life better than I could have ever dreamed of. I would never have chosen the woman I am with, the job I am in, or the place where I am living. The truth for me is that I do not want any choice in my life or love. I could never possibly deliver with my choosing self the same brilliant way that God has done: it would always be from what I liked or didn't like.

The consciousness of love moves so swiftly through matters that have been barriers in the past. I now know what it is to give up my self, not for the sake of the other person, which I could never do before, but for the love that brought us together. It is quite simple, although not always easy. One of the secrets seems to be just enjoying being together and the mutal desire to have nothing between us.

In closing I would like to refer to the myth you speak about which man and woman are able to discover and live. The myth of me, the prince, being united with my princess and living and loving together is a reality in my life. This is something that is happening in another place, another time, yet on earth at the same time through us living our lives together true to love. Nothing is as it seems.

By living what the master says, and eventually by grace, all that I have heard is possible, is coming true.

Thank you for your utter love of God and truth. In love I will always be with thee.

Leon

◆

TRUTH

The truth is nothing.

Dear Barry

I have gained the impression from reading your books and tapes and attending one of your seminars that you are saying, in effect, that 'we' do not exist. Is this true? And if you are saying that we do not exist would this be the same as Advaita or non-dualism?

I would be grateful for a reply so that I can get this straight in my mind.

Harry

Harry

If I have said, 'we do not exist', it would be in a right context and you can seldom separate one statement from the context of statements around it. However, I can say I do not exist as a reality. And I should think that my collective reference would be in that context.

My existence is not a reality, it is a relative reality. And reality can never be relative. For instance every night in deep dreamless sleep I do not exist. This will be in your experience and what is in your experience is the truth. Also, you will note in your experience that when I am in deep dreamless sleep 'we' do not exist and neither does existence exist. As I say, anything that is relative, that changes or that is dependent upon something else, cannot be real. So in that sense we do not exist.

This is not to say or to assume that I am not real. The only question is who am I if I am real? Well, first of all, my reality cannot be my existence because that is all relative. So where in my experience am I real and without existence? In deep dreamless sleep when I know nothing and am nothing and yet find that the most blissful and untroubled state I can at any time recall. From my realisation of the truth, which is universal, I can say that the state of deep dreamless sleep in which I am nothing, is the same as the state before I am born and after I am dead. All that lies between is simply existence which is really my unreality.

Anyway, for me to continue would arouse more questions in you leading to a discussion about such philosophic nonsense as Advaita, non-dualism and the rest of these fancy mindbending or entertaining doctrines.

◆

Dear Barry

What endeavour is more honourable than the quest for God? Who can put his heart to the grindstone and test its metal and valour other than he or she who truly loves the truth? Every moment of my waking hour and all night in my sleep I dwell on the one question that I cannot answer: who am I? Beyond the phenomena, beyond the senses and the mind or the body, even beyond the notion of 'I am' to the source from which all things come.

For me there is no rest and peace is a promise beyond reach. Not because I suffer from this world but because I desire to know that — that which is at and in my heart. There is nothing I would not give to find my beloved. The beloved I have never seen and wish to kiss on the face, for I desire it so and love it in the core of my being.

Barry, why does it elude me so? I hunt ceaselessly like the hunter bent by his overpowering hunger to live. Why does it play hide and seek with my earnestness?

Ralph

Ralph

Who am I? you ask.

You are nothing. But you are holding on to something. You are holding on to the question. You are holding on to the quest for God. You are holding on to the heart, the hide and seek. How can you be nothing when you hold so strenuously to something?

'Barry, why does it (the beloved) elude me so?' Because you keep trying and searching wrongly. You are hoping to gain something when the truth in you, the beloved, is found only in the emptiedness of the heart, only in the being as nothing.

'Seek and you shall find' is one of the great errors of the so-called spiritual path. You must give up seeking, wanting, trying, wishing, hoping — thereby surrendering every action of your own will. When that is done there will be nothing left of you and the beloved will be there.

◆

Dear Barry

I just finished your tape 'The End of the World'. I saw the truth of it, am not concerned about the contents or questioning it, but I am concerned with a matter that is related if not directly involved.

Sir, is not the world and even the earth, sun, moon and sky all the ignorance of who the 'I' is in 'I am'? If the phenomenon is an illusion and the only thing truly is the noumenon (the unknowable), then is not all existence the reflection of my ignorance which I'm seeking to remove and simply be? Or is the phenomenon of the natural earth and everything not made by man, only a reflection and not the ignorance I wish to be rid of?

Roger

Roger

Thank you for your letter. It provided me with another opportunity to endeavour to impart the truth. I trust it helps. It will if you can find something in it to live and not think about.

The earth and everything you see now is a sensory reflection of a reality that can never be understood or described, in other words, interpreted. The reality is real but the reflection — like all reflections — is not real. The sensory reflection, however, does exist and is in fact the continuum of existence. This is more than can be said for the descriptions and interpretations of it. These do not exist. Out of these non-existent ephemeral and purely subjective images arises the movement of the human mind which, being an effect of such aberrations, itself does not exist.

The reality behind the sensory reflection can be realised by the intelligence, I, while in existence. For this, the intelligence, I, has to have lived enough in form, in existence, to have become detached from the world. This means to no longer be attached to the human need to understand, describe or interpret what I am seeing as the sensory reflection. An immediate example of attachment (without the usual apparent emotional element) is the scientific search for explanations of the sensory phenomenon. The sensory phenomenon, I say again, can never be explained. It is what it is, now.

The world is the mind's accumulated interpretation of the sensory reflection. To be attached to a world that is not real is an obvious act of ignorance. Included in this unsuspected global human ignorance is the fear of death. The fear of death is not the fear of losing life. It is the fear of losing the world — the mind and its endless interpretations.

Simply put, as you put it, the earth and all that I see is not my ignorance, for that would be an interpretive word. It is simply what is. Immediately I interpret what is, I am in the world or the world is in me and I soon become discontented and unhappy under the burden of the endless interpretations — the mind-play — of myself and others.

To sum up: in your immediate experience now there are three worlds — really, two states and one condition.

The first state is the reality behind all, so subtle and indescribable that it seems to be nothing. The second state is the immediate physical/sensory reflection (of the reality). And the condition is the great ever-changing and ever-mounting body of human thought and personal thinking which is purely a reflection of human ignorance.

◆

Freedom is a dawning.

Hello Barry

I am facing the prospect of a serious operation involving the removal and replacement of one of my major organs. Since I understand you to say that the body is all we have, I am worried that this transplant might affect my reality.

Also, I have so far not succeeded in overcoming all that is false in me although I live your teaching as earnestly as I am able. It is my greatest desire to achieve the complete destruction of my self before I die.

Jay

Jay

I assure you that no organ transplant can disturb or interfere with your reality of which your body is a transitory sensory projection. Behind the body is your invisible, infinitely subtle, vital being. This is your reality. And although your vital being is relatively perfect, it determines within the scope of the whole of existence what is to happen to, and in, your physical body — when you are to be born and when you are to die and what from. It is this reality that is man's task to endeavour to realise — his own being behind the body. So if you have to have the operation be of good cheer.

Also, it is not a matter of complete destruction of my self but just reducing my self so that I am more and more my pure experience. What we do is attach emotionally to our experience and so think about it and dwell on it emotionally afterwards. But the thing is to let the experience be and to refer to it by speech or thought as little as possible. This reduces my self which normally enjoys thinking and talking about the experience and so enlarges itself. The pure experience, of course, is registered in the body to become something like instinct in the natural creatures. Do you have to think about not touching a hot iron should your hand stray close to it? Of course not. The pure experience is in your body whereas a child, who has not had that experience, will unwittingly burn itself.

Life as you can see it is about experiencing. Whatever experience I draw, somehow, in a profundity deep inside my body, makes me a better man. If you must go through this experience just know that whatever happens it will be okay, you will come through — as you always have up to this moment and always will.

I am with you.

◆

Dear Barry

Your words have had a profound effect on me. While several questions have been cleared up, two still remain:

1. Is it reasonably possible in this life, and in these times, for the individual to detach sufficiently from self in order that freedom might be a constant, or at least near constant, experience of existence?

2. If the answer to the first question is yes, then is the realisation of freedom, and final separation from self, a sudden occurrence or a gradual increase in the realisation until the reality of the situation becomes uninterrupted?

It dawned in this mind some time ago that what is real and true is not in this world, nor an object which can be experienced. Yet at the same time, a knowingness swept over me that dispelled all doubt that what is real, true and beautiful is in Me. It is a clear recognition that everything in the world, including this self, is in time, temporary and limited. And yet these have nothing to do with Me.

I cannot see or know Me in any conventional way because I am not a thing. But when I am just Me, there is happiness in this body and love in this heart. At once, happiness and love are recognised not *as feelings or emotions, but as a real expression that happens when what is real makes contact with existence, as it does through this body. Like light, what is real is invisible and without quality until it comes in contact with a body. Then there is light and warmth; happiness and love. When this knowingness sweeps over me, there are no doubts and I know that God is the source of this light (though unseen) and as his son, happiness and love are my natural birthright.*

But this knowingness doesn't stay. As you pointed out, thoughts arise and some perverse habit takes over. I turn away from happiness which is there in abundance and follow thoughts into time and suffering. Then I feel myself as a person and existence is mean. Is this the usual course of events? Does it have to be this back and forth from knowingness into confusion? At what point is there sufficient clarity and presence to escape the pull of this ingrained habit? Is there any way to just cut it off and walk away once and for all?

I have been using your suggestion of letting emotion fall to the abdomen and just feeling the sensation. I know this is a powerful way to burn off the emotional body and I thank you for that suggestion.

Peter

Peter

Your perceptions, inasmuch as words can convey, are true and I am pleased to read your earnest and intelligent exposition in your letter.

The answer to your first question is yes — with a rider, which I shall add shortly. And the answer to your second question is the latter proposition — freedom is a dawning.

Your intelligence, apart from suggesting the answer, has anticipated the correctness by beginning your next paragraph with the words, 'It dawned in this mind some time ago. . .' There can be sudden and dramatic insights but these are dramatic because they are like a shaft of light thrusting into the dark, the dark being ignorance. These dramatic insights are partial, but dawning is a rising that occurs as an overall dispelling of the dark or ignorance — spiritually the transition from the obscuring dark to the uninterrupted shining of the light.

So you have the knowledge which comes from the uninterrupted dawning you describe in the next three and a half paragraphs of your letter. I repeat, this is your knowledge, not knowing. Knowing, like understanding, arises from the mind and is partial. But knowledge is forever, forever meaning always there, as long as I am not attached to the exercise of knowing or thinking, which you describe well.

The rider to my answer is that there is only self in this existence. And the only liberation from self is when my self is aligned with Me which is the truth outside existence. This alignment is, of course, represented by the age old injunction of surrender to the Most High. In my teaching I endeavour to make surrender more clear by describing it this way. My self's natural propensity, since it is the cause of time, is to move in circles taking its rise from the universal movement of the orbital nature of cosmic bodies. So, as thinking, my self is discursive and moves in circles that under the intensity of gravitation or self-centred emotions, contract into inescapable worry circuits.

As my self aligns with Me, the power of the universe, its circular lines of force start to be straightened — for Me is the power and the glory, and the glory of the power is straight and true. This is the only way to ever escape or resist any selfish or material gravitational pull. As the force of my self becomes aligned with the power of Me, thoughts and the disturbance of perverse habit diminish. Then I, my self in existence, do not and cannot turn away from 'happiness which is there in abundance' and my existence is no longer 'mean'. But the straightening, as you know, is painful.

There is no way I can 'just cut it off and walk away once and for all'. It is, as I say, a dawning resulting from doing all that you have been doing but never overlooking getting your life more right in the external world so that it disturbs you less and less. The external world of circumstances is simply the reflection of myself, aligned and therefore always better, or unaligned and therefore worrisome or confusing.

◆

Dear Barry

I am writing because I know I am living the spiritual life and have started the descent into and through my self. The process started sometime last June when I listened to your 'Who I Am' tape. The tape transformed me.

When I first started going down I had periods of profound peace and sometimes I could sit in the park, or anywhere for that matter, without worry or distress. Hours would pass like minutes.

My point is that I now know my emotions more intimately than ever before. They rise like serpents from the dark within, demanding, wanting, clinging to me like small children afraid of being abandoned. The emotions are less and have less influence on me. However they seem more forceful. I see the emotion rising up and if I can (and I often do), I trap it by centring my attention on my solar plexus as you have suggested and immediately the emotion is completely dissolved or in some cases at least held in check. The emotions seem to have less power but more force from within. Almost as if they are fighting for ground.

Philip

He wrote again two weeks later.

Dear Barry

I am writing to you again in reference to my emotional body. I explained in my last letter that my emotions were getting more pronounced as I endeavoured to centre them on my solar plexus and keep them there.

Well, lately I have had some difficult times doing this. Not because I don't know what I am doing but because my emotions seem to be stronger somehow. It takes every effort on my part at times to keep them in the solar plexus where (as you have stated) they can become dissolved. I have been successful up to this point, holding them there and dissolving them.

The part that puzzles me is that the emotions rise from situations where I would have normally expressed them in some long dreadful speech or some emotional outburst after which I would return to my normal state. Now that I am successfully endeavouring to contain them, at least for some time in my solar plexus, they seem simply over-powering in their strength against my efforts and I have noticed that since I try not to let them up into my brain, the emotional body seems more real and alive than ever.

Could you please help clarify this situation for me?

Philip

Philip

As you said in your first letter the emotions seem more forceful but have less power. That's how it works. You are the power and as you gain more power (consciousness) over your self, the self or emotions become more threatened and desperate. They can't get out and express themselves as in the past in long speeches or anger.

You have contained them in the solar plexus. I suggest that now you contain them in your entire body. This will give you extra power, for the whole body is a whole consciousness. To do this you will have a sense of broadness in the body. Don't panic and feel you have no edge to contain the emotions. Your whole body is the containment. This can only be done when you have truly worked and succeeded at centring in the solar plexus as you have.

Your 'brain' is not a part of your body. The brain you refer to is really the field of the emotional mind and that is outside the body. The whole spiritual exercise is not to allow the emotions/thoughts to go outside. This teaching focuses on bringing everything in the field back in the body. Hence what I have now written.

Don't doubt. And don't try. Be easy. Know the new broadness or vastness that is possible. And, anyway, what are you emotional about? Have you attended to that source of disturbance?

◆

Dear Barry

In your teaching I have found much authenticity and some great parallels to my own experience of being human. Ten years ago I had an experience which from my present vantage seems extraordinary, but at the time was utterly ordinary. I suddenly just simply was. I was no one yet I was me. There was no emotion, no joy, no sorrow. My thinking was totally clear and I had no desire. I was not identified with gender or personality: both had fallen away. I was simply the being in this location. I was alive yet dead to human emotion. Sentient emotions had washed out of my body and I was in a 'timeless' condition. I was cognisant of being in a place/state/condition that probably others had been in before me but I thought that if I remained there and went amongst people, they would be impelled to harm my body or run from my 'self' — as if my neutrality would be a vacuum to their personalities.

Thinking that having 'gotten' to this stage I would be able to come back, I chose to return to my humanity because I sensed (not felt) a child in me who was 'meant' to be in existence. Something was incomplete and, paradoxically, it was all irrelevant. So I sat on my bed again and called back and allowed my emotions to wash back in to me — my body, psyche, self. What I remember next is a fulfilling feeling of love and benevolence. I was new and sure and complete.

I haven't been able to regain that state. I know it is here now, yet I am out here. But in your tapes and the one book I've read, I've sensed an inherent likeness or ontological agreement and also things which are divergent. Somehow I

*feel that what you are and have been through is similar to
my experience — just interpreted differently here and there.*

Joe

Joe

Your description of your realisation of what it is to simply
be now is one of the finest that I have read. So was your
description of how you allowed your emotions to wash
back into you and you lost the pristine state, despite a fulfilling feeling of love and benevolence, newness and
completion, before it disappeared. It disappeared because
you flirted with your emotions, thinking the state could
be maintained in their presence. That is an error made by
many people having such realisations.

The state, as you say, is there now covered over by
those same emotions or self. Since it is there (and always
there) all you have to do is give up self-consideration and
the feelings that go with that sort of selfishness. You do
that now. And since now is every moment, once done
now, it is done for every now.

Two months later he wrote again.

Barry

*Thank you for your reply to my letter and especially for your
thoughts regarding the loss of the 'pristine state'. I did not*

think that the state could be maintained in the presence of my emotions. I knew that it was by emergence from emotion that I realised this impersonal state of desireless clarity.

I was utterly still in presence and I sensed that others wouldn't be able to be near me because I was the death of who they thought they were. I was the non-existence of the personality. I saw in my thoughts that they would become alarmed, fearful and confused and would either run from me or try to harm me. There was no-one to share this state and its accompanying thoughts/realisations with. This is one reason why I did not remain there. Also I reasoned that, as it was something I could return to, I would re-enter the 'human' world and live for the unfulfilled, incomplete little boy in me who loved others and wanted to be alive. 'Armed/equipped' with the realisation I had had, I expected to be successful. Needless to say, I failed. It has taken me years to see that I cannot live for the little boy. I must live to live and be true.

Barry, you also know that this 'pristine state', this point of view and excellent vantage is always there/here. And in your letter you said that to return to this utter nowness of now, all I 'have to do is give up self-consideration and the feelings that go with that sort of selfishness'. I will do this but I request some clarification: I'm not sure what you mean by 'self-consideration'. Would you be more specific and define self-consideration as you use the term? Also, what is 'that sort of selfishness'? What are the feelings that go with it? It would help if I could name them. How can I give up this self-consideration?

Joe

Joe

Self-consideration is consideration of your self. Your self consists of all your past emotional hurts, disappointments and sexual traumas since you were born.

Whenever you consider any emotional feeling you are considering your self. For instance if you ever think or feel you are a failure, you are self-considering. If you ever think or feel disappointed, moody, depressed, resentful, angry or just plain unhappy, you are considering your self.

I suggest that you read some of my books and listen to my tapes. These will give you a comprehensive instruction in my teaching and the terms that I use. These terms, I have to say, are correct and not just something that describes my particular use of them. It seems the world has no knowledge of what self is and for that reason you are forced to ask, 'what is self-consideration?'

Also you ask me what is 'that sort of selfishness' associated with self. The word selfish (not my invention) obviously comes from self and selfish people are selfish. Since self is all negative and therefore destructive of your happiness and those around you, if it is considered, it is the very essence of selfishness. Instead of being open to the beauty of life at those times and radiating the goodness of that state, you contract into an aspect of your self and shut off from the good of the whole which is the good of being.

◆

Be the king, the master of your self.

Dear Barry

Thank you for the Master Session and for making yourself so available. It was a very powerful experience for me and I had a greater realisation of many of the things you have been saying. Many distinctions became clearer for me, deepening my being with Me and reducing my self.

Since the Master Session I've become increasingly aware of the many aspects of self and of the energy drain that occurs when self is indulged.

I've seen my self-absorption, the self's wilfulness, the self-righteousness, the need for acknowledgement, the duality of self-aggrandisement and inferiority, the considerations that prevent me from giving, the fear and feelings of unworthiness which in recent years have prevented me from being as open to you and from being able to communicate freely with you.

In facing my self I've gone through a range of feelings — discomfort, shame, despair, hopelessness, unworthiness — which I recognise as representing more self.

How can I deal with the self that seeks approval? This seems to me to result from my identification with the shame of self rather than being with Me. Isn't everyone self-obsessed to some degree? Do you see something in me that I'm not seeing in my self?

Anthony

Anthony

First of all an acknowledgment, whether you're looking for it or not. You are earnest in your spiritual endeavour and you will always be earnest, whatever you do.

From your letter I am reminded of my tape 'The Truth of Self'. You should listen to it. You are nicely along the way to realising self, although it is, as I say in the tape, a process in the life that lasts many years, if not the whole life. I think you might have the realisation as a climacteric well before you die, which is quite a thing in existence.

You will notice from your letter that it is all about seeing your self in its various aspects. This is necessary, a vital part of the process. You cannot really have a measure of it because it is being done for you and any estimate that you would make would be an estimate of self, and therefore self-delusion. But I can tell you the process of knowing yourself, through facing yourself, is at the same time the reduction of self and the separating from it.

Finally self is perceived as a whole and this means that the perceiver, I, am not my self — quite an amazing realisation.

You ask if I have any suggestions and then your self suggests that the problem is that you are identifying with the basic shame of self etc. You have put your finger on the solution. You *must not* go into your feelings any more. From this moment, there is no justification for you considering how you feel. Your feelings have nothing to teach you, nothing to inform you of except that they are there, like a psychic channeller, waiting for you to give them your attention so that they can possess you, take your intelligence over. You must stay in your senses, which is the only

reality, until you are strong enough in that reality to stay
with the constant being of Me within — as distinct from the
vacillating feelings of the self. By refusing to consider, to
think about or try to understand your self, your feelings,
you will solve every other problem mentioned in your letter.

Now to your two last questions. Last one first. It's not a
question of what you're not seeing. It's a question of what
you are doing that you must not do — do not consider
your self. Now the first question: there is only self in existence, so in that sense everybody is self-obssessed since
every body is self, the natural body made by God. There
are only bodies in existence, no other self. The feeling
selfish self is out of existence in an intermediate hellish
world made by man's thoughts and emotions without any
reality, except that it influences existence for what is not
good, destroying the peace of the natural self and the
natural creativity and life of the earth. So, since every body
— just about — has the pain of past hurt and the ignorance
of man's notions in its subconscious, the simple thing to
do to be free is not to enter this hellish half world of your
own feelings, your hurt and hurtful self.

A year later he wrote again.

Barry

I think I finally got it.
I think this is it.
I have realised what I am, that I am not my self and
that, for my whole life, I have been identified with my self

as what I am — and have been attempting to become what I already am. How ridiculous. I have realised my stupidity. I have woken up out of my dream.

I never left home.

The goose was never in the bottle.

I am already in the room which I always wanted to enter. What I am is nothing, the container of all things. What I am is not even dependent on any particular experience of being. When I realised that, that's when I really got it.

I feel tremendously blessed, Barry, and my self is astounded. It finally gave up and God blessed me for giving up. What a joke. Who would ever believe it? Although everything is the same to a degree, it is all completely different. I am free.

Anthony

◆

Dear Barry

Eight years on and I'm still at it — living the truth, within and without, as much as I'm consciously able. It isn't easy, but it isn't hard either. All it takes is willingness and the increasing ability to be conscious in any situation.

I look into Me. It is still. It is wondrous. It is beyond my description and I'm grateful for ever being able to perceive it and be it. Reciprocally my life without is made easier. Situations lose their previous tension and I'm able to handle them more easily.

However, in becoming more conscious within, I see that in perceiving the good, I necessarily become more conscious of the 'phantom' within me — my self. These few months I have felt as though I'm burning inside as the phantom tries its damndest to distract me, while I endeavour to be still and contain it. One of its tricks is to give me a physical problem such as pain, confusion and a dizziness that had me going to various doctors to get some relief. None of them could do anything effective because they don't know the cause. I couldn't tell them for they don't know what I'm talking about.

So it's back to me, looking into Me, containing the pain with the good and it is all right. I've got some dying to do before I'm through this hell of mine. The thing is, despite being afflicted by this phantom, deep within, when I do reach it, life is beautiful. Oh God, I can't even begin to describe this beauty, but you know what I'm talking about.

One thing I notice is, while the affliction continues within to persuade me to stop being real, people and events outside are also conspiring to persuade me to stop what I'm doing. I've been told by well-meaning people to rejoin them in their world of ignorance, their religions, beliefs and hopes for a better future. I couldn't. It's like what you said once about climbing my own mountain towards the pinnacle. Ignorance disguised as fun and games is still ignorance and it all ends with death, which terrifies the ignorant.

So I climb on, not knowing how high it is to the top. The initial fear is no more. I'm going up. The wonderful thing is that climbing needs no effort. The effort is the phantom trying to drag me down, to immerse myself again in it. I give up the effort and, by God, life is simple.

But if you do see me being wilful through what I've written, do give me a kick in the butt, so to speak, so that I do not slide back into ignorance.

Damien

Damien

It was pleasing to hear from you again and to read your descriptions of how right the living of the truth within and without is for you. I don't see anything amiss in what you say. I'm delighted to hear you say it.

You probably know about the Master Session which is now held each year in northern New South Wales, where I speak to attendees over sixteen days. If you could manage to attend, the contact with me over the extended time would be good for you and affirm what you have been doing.

A month later Damien wrote again

Dear Barry

It is my pleasure and privilege to hear from you. Thank you.

I shall endeavour to come to the Master Session this year. However that depends on whether my health holds out. At present I can't even walk ten metres without feeling as though I'm going to fall. My sense of balance is disturbed. You see, I have declared to life, as you have suggested, to take anything from me — health, possessions, anything that I hold dear. And I have not declared it in jest. Thus I can now perceive life working on me, taking away things which I am attached to, often painfully. I can't complain for I have asked life to do it. I am responsible. So I face whatever comes, every moment.

At the moment I am pinned to the ground like a defeated wrestler. I learn the meaning of surrender to life. I learn the meaning of giving up wanting and trying. I learn not to jump up again and pursue the world which I was tempted to do. All that is left is this residue of emotions that I've not got rid of, and it is wriggling and struggling to regain control of me. Of course I can't allow that, thus the pain of its death. I shall go through all of this hell and I have the only means available — stillness. This is of course what you have said all along, but it is no longer just what you said. It is reality for me. When I am cleaned out, you will know of it.

Thank you.

Damien

Damien

I have your last letter and there is something very important
I want to say to you.

I suggest that the continuing failure in your health
and mobility, as you describe it, is being caused by what
has now become a rigidly determined, a somewhat
wilful attempt to overcome the residual emotions or self
you perceive in you. I want you to receive, please, my
knowledge (for examination in your own experience),
that your (or anyone's) constant, diligent practical living
of the truth after so many years is likely to become a
retrogressive activity.

In the beginning, and possibly for years, it is a virtuous
way of life that inexorably does what it's supposed to do,
reduce the self. But all things have an end, even the
struggles and effort of the spiritual life. And there comes
a time when the job is done and any further perseverance
will have a deleterious effect, as in stuffing yourself with
food after the appetite is filled.

The emotional self can never be killed and it is not
supposed to be. This whole existence is self and I speak
and am writing to you now through my self. The self
indeed has to be mastered and I say that you have done
this. And in saying, 'I am pinned to the ground like a
defeated wrestler', you are speaking the truth. But it is not
I, the holy one, the intelligence in your body that is
defeated: it is your self. You are rightly identifying with
your self when you say that, for as I say, you are your self
and you know you are defeated. The purpose of this
defeat, even though by habit you may not be able to

accept that the match is over, is to align your self with Me, the intelligence, the holy one in that body. So defeated, utterly surrendered, the self awaits the unspoken command of the master that has wrestled it into submission. That's how it is for you now.

When the fight is over, to persist in wrestling the defeated one activates a force of divine indignation which will result in a continuous debilitating effect.

So, Damien, I am asking you to stop. Give up now. Release the pressure. Be magnanimous. Be the king, the master of your system, and allow your self to now serve you as the loving disciple. Due to your spiritual efforts you now have a superb presence of power and stillness. Your self knows this without knowing how. You have shown it, by never giving in, that you are the master of spiritual endurance. Take your knee off the defeated one's throat. Let it arise and serve you.

There is a story in Nietzsche's book, 'Thus Spake Zarathustra'. I'm not sure what he intended but this is the way I see it in regard to the spiritual life. During his period of self-denial, Zarathustra looked around him, despised the ignorance of the people in the market place and took off to the mountain top with his eagle and his lion, to live above it all.

After a long period of isolation he was moved to go down the mountain again with his eagle and his lion. His eagle was his intelligence, and his lion his courage. So back among the people and into the marketplace he went in the company of his eagle and his lion, untouchable and unaffected by the ignorance around him. He knew that was the way it was, and that his place was to walk there talking and mixing with the people, inspecting their handiworks, smiling in appreciation, exchanging a few words here and there, but never lingering for long with anyone or in any place unless so moved to do.

It is time. You have been given by grace the eagle and the lion. It is not for yourself in isolation. It is for Me, humanity. Wherever you go, have no goal to teach. Just be. Those who have a question will ask. There is no need to change anything. You will be led without being led.

◆

Works mentioned in the text

The following works by Barry Long have been mentioned in the text.

Journal Volume Two
Covering the period from early 1990 to the end of 1991 the three volumes of Barry Long's Journal are a record of his daily musings and penetrating observations of the truth behind the changing world of events and circumstances.

Meditation A Foundation Course
A straightforward way of meditation taught step by step in ten lessons, using a down-to-earth approach with practical exercises to apply in everyday life. Barry Long discards the religious, occult or psychic traditions associated with meditation in the past.

Stillness Is The Way
This book is a record of three days of teaching by Barry Long. It follows the process experienced by several people as he teaches them over the course of two weekends, steadily going deeper into meditation and undoing the resistance of the mind.

To Woman In Love
A book of letters about love, its pain and transcending beauty, written to Barry by women in different countries. His replies are intimate, challenging and compassionate.

242 TO MAN IN TRUTH

KNOWING YOURSELF

This book challenges the reader to find what lies behind the appearance of things. Barry Long begins with focusing on the fact of our experience then strips away one layer of self-delusion after another, until at the end there is nothing but pure perception and the being of God.

MAKING LOVE

A two-tape set which teaches man and woman to make love rightly, dealing with the source of sexual unhappiness; the true myth of love; emotionality and how to get rid of it; sexual problems and how to resolve them; the secrets of lovemaking; the way to find the passion and consciousness of making love divine.

START MEDITATING NOW

Part of a two-tape set with How To Stop Thinking, this is a practical step-by-step instruction in meditation. Barry explains why you need to meditate, how to stop thought and deal with worry. He gives exercises to release tension and dissolve emotion and shows how to let go of resentment and get in touch with life.

WHO I AM

The fundamental question, 'Who am I?' examined in three steps of self-knowledge: the true use of logic; how consciousness is made; the actuality of what I am.

THE END OF THE WORLD

A prayer to life, challenging illusions and affirming the reality of life.

The Truth Of Self
This tape demonstrates what the self is and what self-realisation is.

The Course In Being
The title of Barry Long's international teaching program from 1991 to 1995. Since 1996 his meetings are simply entitled Being with Barry Long.

The Master Session
A sixteen day event, the Master Session is the annual culmination of Barry Long's international teaching program. He covers a vast area of the spiritual life and the extended period gives a deep grounding in truth and love so that participants can apply it in their daily lives. The Master Session is held at Cabarita Beach in northern New South Wales in Australia.

◆

Details of Barry Long's books, tapes and teaching program may be obtained from:

The Barry Long Foundation International
via the following addresses:

England ~ BCM Box 876, London WC1N 3XX

Australia ~ Box 5277, Gold Coast MC, Queensland 4217

USA ~ 6230 Wilshire Boulevard Suite 251, Los Angeles, CA 90048 *or call* 1-800-497-1081

SUBJECT GUIDE

Attachment, 4, 7
  to pain, 109-112
  to past, 30
Attraction, 96-99

Being, state of, 224-225
Being true, 70, 94-98
Betrayal, 55

Effort, 20-21, 47-48
Emotion
  containment of, 6, 221-223
  detachment from, 38-40
  dissolving, 137-138
  flirting with, 225
  giving up, 3-4
  taking responsibility for, 7-8
Enlightenment, 17-18

Facing the fact/life as it is, 82-83,
  141-142
Family
  caring for sick spouse, 82-83
  familiarity in, 78-79
  mother problem, 114
  true love in, 79
Feelings, 231-233
Freedom, 217-220
Friendship, 120-121

Getting your life right, 3-5, 21, 56-57
Gnosis, 24
God
  love of, 106, 141-142
  quest for, 207-208
Gratitude, 37-38, 65-66
Guardian of the Threshold, 154
Guilt, 116-117

Honesty before love, 7-8

Independence, 132-133

Jealousy, 139-142
Journal Two, 20

Knowing Yourself, 29
Knowledge and knowing, 219
Kundalini, 23, 25

Life is good, 63-64
Love
  acknowledgement of, 185-186
  fear of, 99-100
  honesty in, 122-123
  loss of, 141-142
  realisation of, 189-197
  service in, 83
  waiting for, 91-92
Loving God first, 70-71
Loving two women, 126-131
Lust, getting rid of, 8-10

Making love, 126-127, 163-165,
  183-184
  lack of response in, 185
  healing woman's pain, 170-171
  inability to get erection, 157-158
  man's orgasm, 170-171
  post-coital tristesse, 172-174
  premature ejaculation, 175-177
  purpose of, 11
  seminal retention, 23, 25
  using a condom, 168-169
  woman's disinterest in, 163-165
Making Love tapes, 157-158, 164,
  170, 183

Male menopause, 50
Manhood, fear of losing, 133
Masturbation, 116-117, 150-151,
   157-160
Meditation, 29-38
Meditation A Foundation Course,
   29
Money
   earning, 49-51
   management of, 52-54, 56-57

Noble man, 11-12

Pain, of the past, 72-75, 109-112
Partnership
   commitment in, 110-112
   conflict in, 118-119
   ending of, 122-123
   fathering a child, 69-70
Payment for meetings, 56-57
Pornography, 155-156
Prostitutes, visiting, 159-160
Purpose of life, 17-19

Raja Yoga, 35-36
Realisation
   of God, 39-40
   of love, 189-197
   of self, 27-28, 231-24
Reality behind existence, 205-
   206, 209-211, 215
Rejection, 98

Self, 5-7, 58-59
   alignment of, 219-220, 238-239
   consideration of, 98, 225-227
   dissolving of, 39-40
   facing emotional past of, 153-
   154
   giving up for love, 191-192
   liberation from, 217-219
   mastery of, 237-240

negation of, 126-127
   reducing, 215-216
   struggle of, 47-48
Self-doubt, 94-98
Sensuality and sexuality, 166-167
Sexual
   addiction, 159
   excitement, getting rid of, 8-11
   fantasies, 9, 150-154
   magic, 23- 26
   wanting, 147-149
Spiritual power, 5
Start Meditating Now, 29
Stillness Is The Way, 29, 150
Suicide, 80-81

Taking woman on, 10-11
The End of the World, 209
The Truth of Self, 232
The witness, 20-22
The world, doing what is
   required, 45-46
Thinking, 20-22
To Woman In Love, 33-34
Transcendental Meditation, 35-
   37, 82, 84-85
Trust, 55

Who I Am, 221
Woman
   approaching, 94-98
   fear of, 99-105
   God in female form, 8, 181
   man's love of, 101-102, 106
   longing for love of, 32-34, 91-98
   loving of, 8-11, 147-149
   reflection of man's virtue, 81
Wooing, 92-93, 98, 185-186
Work, 4, 43-44, 49-51, 58-59

Youth, 29-34